Choosing Faith

Choosing Faith

The Importance of Belief in Finding Purpose in Life

JOHN W. SAULTZ

RESOURCE *Publications* • Eugene, Oregon

CHOOSING FAITH
The Importance of Belief in Finding Purpose in Life

Resource Publications
An Imprint of Wipf and Stock Publishers
199 W. 8th Ave., Suite 3
Eugene, OR 97401

www.wipfandstock.com

PAPERBACK ISBN: 978-1-5326-7470-9
HARDCOVER ISBN: 978-1-5326-7471-6
EBOOK ISBN: 978-1-5326-7472-3

Manufactured in the U.S.A.   APRIL 18, 2019

To the love of my life: my wife, Sherrie;

To my children: David, Jennifer, and Andy
and their spouses Alisha, Byron, and Jenny;

To my grandchildren: Derek, Will, Sharon, Alison,
Maya, JD, and Alexander;

And to the patients who have shared their life stories with me
over the past forty years.

"Your purpose in life is to find your purpose
and give your whole heart and soul to it"

—BUDDHA

Contents

Preface

Beliefs can be highly personal, and discussions about faith can easily come across as advocacy for a predetermined point of view. My goal in this book is not to convince you to believe what I believe. That being said, context is important, and it will not help the process if you read the book while trying to guess what my beliefs are as the author. So I offer here a brief overview of my personal perspective in hopes that it will help you to make sense of what is to follow.

I was born in a small town in Ohio, and my sister and I were raised in a two-parent family in the Lutheran Church. My parents were married for 62 years. My father was a civil service government employee, and my mother was a housewife. I attended public school and went to college on an Army ROTC scholarship to study mathematics. After college, I attended medical school and served in the army for seven years as an army physician. At the start of medical school, I married my high school sweetheart. We met when we were 16 years old, and have been together ever since. We have been married 43 years and have three children and seven grandchildren.

After medical school, I completed a residency in family medicine and have spent the last 35 years as a medical school faculty member. I teach physicians to be rural and small-town family doctors, and I study the importance of continuity in doctor-patient relationships. As a practicing family physician, I care for people of all ages and genders. I deliver babies and care for people who are dying. My work brings me into close contact with people with problems and affords me daily opportunities to witness the human condition.

My wife, my family, and my profession are the three greatest blessings in my life. My wife is a person of strong faith and has been an ideal life partner for me. I have learned much from the experience of raising three children and watching my children and their spouses raise children of their own. My career affords me the privilege of being trusted by people as their family physician. In this capacity, they share their stories, their fears, and their hopes with me. I have seen people at their best and at their worst. I have cared for people who are happy and people who are angry. I have delivered babies and cared for them into adulthood and have a special interest in how families grow and change over time. Being a physician gives me a front-row seat into how people live their lives, many of whom are very different from me. Being a physician has taught me to avoid judging others, even when I disagree strongly with the choices they make or the values they espouse.

Over the course of my life, my faith has become more and more important to me. I am an active Christian and member of a Lutheran Church, but I am also a scientist and a humanist, and I believe that education and life-long learning are important. I believe in the American form of government. I believe in the scientific method and the use of formal logic to prove mathematical theorems. I believe in the importance of family and community. I tend to see the work of God in nature and in the hearts of human beings, but I have worked closely with colleagues of widely different backgrounds and perspectives. Thus I believe that I can learn much from those who hold different beliefs than my own.

Writing a book about beliefs is not possible without first acknowledging that my own experiences and beliefs form the foundation for how I think about things. It is only fair that I start by sharing these perspectives. But now we need to set them aside and start from the beginning.

Introduction

What do you believe? Do you have faith in a deity or religion, a philosophy, a system of core principles, or perhaps in certain people: your partner, your children, your role models? We all believe in something, whether we recognize it or not, and our beliefs are foundational to our lives. Sometimes, we believe in other people, putting our trust in them to love us, to look out for our best interests, and to stay with us through the hard times. Sometimes, we believe in political ideas or scientific principles, such as democracy, or the scientific method, or the rules of mathematics. We believe that the light will turn on when we flip the switch, the chair will hold our weight when we sit down, and the plane will safely land at the end of our flight. Beliefs are not things we can prove, but we believe them to be true, and so we build our lives around them.

Goals

The goal of this book is to help the reader to think deeply about his or her beliefs and to explore how we develop and use our system of beliefs as we make decisions in our lives. It is about moral growth and development and about the importance of faith for each of us, regardless of what the specifics of that faith might be. *Faith* is not used here in a purely religious sense, but instead refers to the development and use of a system of values we choose to trust in making both momentous and ordinary life decisions. Faith can be organized or disorganized. It can be weak or strong. Our decisions can be consistent or inconsistent. We start by making no presumptions about the importance of any particular belief system. The book is not about why one faith system might be better than others. We will, however, address how we develop beliefs and how we learn over time about which to retain and which to reject or modify. Today, people sometimes equate belief with superstition as though faith was a phase we move through as we acquire knowledge about the world, eventually replacing our beliefs with this knowledge. But this book instead takes the position that acquiring knowledge is not really possible if we believe in nothing. After all, why acquire knowledge if we do not believe that knowledge makes life better?

Most books about religious faith start with the question of God. Is there a God? What is God's nature? This book eventually gets to these questions but instead starts with what it means to believe anything and why believing matters. Once we can agree that belief is important, we can begin to explore what to believe.

Vocabulary

For this book to make sense, we will need to agree on some basic definitions. Which of the following statements does not belong with the other three?

a. In my opinion, Mary is a smart person.

b. I think that Mary is a smart person.

c. I know Mary is a smart person.

d. I believe Mary is a smart person.

In the everyday use of language, we might consider these statements to mean pretty much the same thing. All of them are clear first-person statements indicating the writer's assessment about whether or not a specific person, Mary, is smart. But if we read the statements carefully, it is clear they do not say exactly the same thing. The first statement does not actually make a claim about Mary at all. It simply states an opinion. Nothing is required to prove this statement. Since we cannot read the writer's mind, there is no way to know if the statement is true or false. The second statement makes a claim about Mary. If someone makes this statement to us, we are inclined to ask why he or she thinks so, but the second statement is still a lot like the first. We do not necessarily require the reasons to be convincing. The writer is expressing a thought, and this is not very different from expressing an opinion. If a writer makes the third statement, he or she is making the point more forcefully. To say that you know something to be true means more than to say you think it is true. Knowing implies that convincing reasons exist. What about the fourth statement? In everyday use, people might consider the fourth statement to be pretty much the same as the first two. For the purposes of this book, statement four is different.

Knowing something means being certain it is true based on observation, experience, reliable information sources, or logical deduction. There is an entire field of study in philosophy, epistemology, which is devoted to the study of knowledge and how it is acquired. Some of the great minds in history have struggled with questions related to knowledge and their lack of consensus suggests this is a very complex subject indeed.[1] *Belief* also eludes easy definition. Some people define a belief as something we think is true but cannot demonstrate or prove. In essence, they consider thinking something to be the same thing as believing it and they consider both thinking and believing to imply a lesser degree of certainty than knowing. Others would consider a belief to be something we do not know but assume to be true. For them, thinking and believing are different.

If you consult a dictionary, you will find *belief* defined as a firmly held opinion.[2] You might also find a definition that a belief is something we accept to be true without proof. In general, most

1. Moser, *The Oxford Handbook of Epistemology.*
2. *New Oxford American Dictionary*,152.

definitions make two distinctions between *belief* and *opinion*. The first is a difference in conviction. Stating we believe something carries more weight than simply stating that we have an opinion about it. The second difference is in importance. A *belief* in something implies that the matter is more important in some way than just having an opinion. Missing from these definitions of belief is a connection between what we believe and what we decide to do. If the connection between belief and action is not made explicit, then it would seem we can do whatever we want regardless of our beliefs.

So, for the purposes of this book, a *belief* is something we cannot prove, but choose to accept as true when making decisions and choices in our lives. We might say that we think something when we are not sure enough to say we know it. We would say we believe something when we assume its truth and make decisions accordingly. As you consider this definition, you might choose to focus on the lack of proof as evidence that believing is somehow less significant than knowing. Alternatively, because our beliefs form a foundation for our decisions, perhaps believing in things is more important than knowing them. Viewing these concepts in scientific terms, thinking something is true is like having a hypothesis. It is plausible but not yet proven. Knowing requires proof. Believing, then, is like a postulate. Euclid created the field of geometry by starting with five postulates. While these postulates cannot be proven, they form the foundation for everything else in the field. Changing one of the postulates changes all of the rest of geometry. In fact, Euclid's fifth postulate, the so-called parallel postulate, can be changed to create entirely new mathematical systems, often called non-Euclidean geometries. So a postulate cannot be proven; it is assumed as a starting point for understanding what truth is. Scientists might have a hypothesis that the orbits of planets are elliptical. They might then conduct observations or experiments to prove this hypothesis, afterward concluding that they know this to be true. But the scientist *believes* in the scientific method as a way of carrying out that proof. Their belief is based on a trust that systematic observation and experimentation will reveal truth. Is there a difference between believing something and believing in it? Perhaps this is just a matter of semantics. In common use we tend to reserve "believe in" for situations when we are talking about trust in people or important principles while we use "believe" when referring to simpler matters. In this book, the terms will be used interchangeably.

Individual beliefs do not exist in a vacuum. Belief in the scientific method fits into a larger system of beliefs related to the capacity of human beings to understand the universe in rational terms. *Faith* is a system of related beliefs that form a foundation for making life decisions. This would certainly include religious faith, but would also include other systems of belief such as believing in democracy or the principles of human rights outlined in the United States Constitution. Considered in this way, beliefs are about our values while knowledge is about factual or theoretical information.

A belief may not be provable, but beliefs cannot be based on information that is provably false. This raises the question of how we "know" when a belief is false and what evidence should be considered when determining what is provably false. Thus, some people would distinguish between a true belief and a false belief in this way. One might also argue that a false belief is really just an error or delusion and not a belief at all. Thus, we will avoid using the term "false belief." Beliefs are not worth much if we give up on them easily, but retaining false beliefs in the face of contradictory evidence causes faulty decision making, sometimes with catastrophic results. So beliefs might not be permanent. They should be reexamined over time and this process is healthy and essential.

A *belief* cannot be proven true or false while genuine *knowledge* must be based on convincing evidence. What sort of evidence are we talking about? What do we mean by convincing? Most people would agree that we can know things if we have direct personal experience that they are true. A rose smells fragrant and a skunk smells acrid. Sugar tastes sweet and a lemon tastes sour. We know these things because we can directly experience them by observation through our senses. And we tend to believe that our five senses give us an accurate picture of reality, even though they can sometimes be fooled. We can also know things when we can derive them by the use of logic. We know that two plus three is five and not four by using the commonly accepted rules of arithmetic. We believe in the rules of logic and use them as tests for mathematical proofs. We can know things because we learned them from a source of information we trust. We know that Abraham Lincoln was president during the Civil War because we can find this information in dependable history textbooks. We believe that textbooks are accurate and trust them to be true. Finally, we can know something if a trustworthy person tells us it is so. It is this last form of knowing that is the basis for both the knowledge and the beliefs of children. We learn that things are true when our parents or other adults tell us so. It is only later that we learn that they might not actually be true at all.

Outline of the Book

This book is organized into ten chapters separated into four sections. The first section explains how beliefs are learned and developed from childhood into adolescence and adulthood. Beliefs change over time and this happens as part of normal growth and development from birth to death. Beliefs often start as social constructs and become internalized over time. Because we have defined a belief as a determinant of behavior, the notion of *integrity* as a characteristic of adult faith is emphasized. There is also an introduction to the costs and risks of our beliefs.

The second section of the book explores different types of belief and the boundaries between opinion, knowledge, and belief. Beliefs occur within a context and have both a conditional and a probabilistic dimension. The second section concludes with an in-depth discussion of moral and religious beliefs including a brief introduction to the history of these concepts.

The third section examines in more detail the process by which beliefs change over time and includes a brief introduction to the techniques of marketing and propaganda that are used by others to change our beliefs. The final section of the book deals with collections of beliefs as systems of faith and introduces the notion that some beliefs are given higher priorities in our lives. Our most strongly held beliefs constitute our primary guides in making important life decisions; so how we assign their relative importance matters. Finally, we emphasize that beliefs are ultimately our own choices to make and the process of making these choices and living accordingly impacts the courses of our lives profoundly.

In general, the book will be most useful if read from start to finish. To the greatest extent possible, the reader should read each chapter while considering his or her own beliefs and experience. The book is not about what you should or should not believe. Instead, it is intended to help you think about why you believe what you do and how you can know if and when your beliefs should be modified or changed.

PART I

Building a Belief System

"One person with a belief is worth ninety-nine people who have only interests."

—John Stuart Mill[1]

---

1. Goodreads, Belief Quotes.

I

The Faith of Children

Almost everything we learn in life starts when we are children. Most of us learn things from parents or other adult role models and then from our teachers. As we get older, we learn from peers and from books and other forms of media. Learning to believe in something starts as early as learning to walk or talk. But even as children, we are confronted with a distinction between knowing something and believing it. Children learn not to throw food at the table when adults tell them this is inappropriate, and they learn to associate rewards and punishment with following and not following behavioral rules. In essence, they learn from experience and therefore *know* that there will be consequences for breaking the rules. But following these rules is not the same thing as believing in them. Behavior guided by rewards and punishment depends on external controls. At some point in time, however, the behavior becomes internalized; we do not throw food at the table even when no one is looking. Thus, a behavior becomes a value and we go from knowing the rule to believing in it.

Role Models and Stories

Just as testimony from a reliable person forms the foundation of what children know, it is also the foundation of what they believe. Most young children in America believe in Santa Claus, the Tooth Fairy, or the Easter Bunny. They are told that these things exist by their parents or other adult role models and they make choices to send letters to Santa Claus or put lost teeth under their pillows based on these beliefs. Do parents know that Santa Claus exists? Can parents prove that Santa Claus exists? No, but perhaps they think that believing in Santa Claus brings joy to children and families. So children learn beliefs from parents just as they learn rules of behavior. As these children grow older, they not only look for Christmas gifts under the tree; they also buy Christmas gifts for their parents and siblings. They make decisions and take action based on a belief in Santa Claus even though they may modify this belief as they get older into a belief in the "spirit of Christmas."

Testimony is a foundational source of both knowledge and belief in children. Just as children learn to believe in Santa Claus, they also learn to believe in God, or not. When parents take their children to church or synagogue, or mosque, the children learn that other adults also believe in God. Being part of a group that believes in something becomes the foundation of what the child believes, and this form of belief is usually pretty much unquestioned by young children. They believe because they are part of the family or part of a church group and the issue of how to establish the truth of this belief is left for later.

Another aspect of the belief of children relies on stories. Just as religious texts are full of stories that constitute morality tales, so are books of fairy tales and children's literature. These stories are ways to exemplify the difference between right and wrong, good and bad, noble and disgraceful. Stories are powerful ways to teach and to learn for all ages, but they are particularly powerful for children because children are uniquely adept at inserting themselves into the stories they are told. As a child learns to read and encounters movies and other types of media, the impact of stories expands and they develop an inner world of make believe that contributes to the formation of their values. Children do not need to believe that Cinderella existed to learn from the story that humility and hard work are good, and that greed and jealousy are bad. So stories provide important support for the testimony of adult role models and parents. The child learns facts about the world, but they also learn a system of values or beliefs; they develop a faith. Intellectual development is connected to moral development in this way.

Rules, Rewards, and Punishment

We started this discussion by considering the way children learn not to throw food at the dinner table. This learning starts with rules and the rules become associated with rewards when the rule is followed and punishment when it is not. Children that throw food might be excused from the table without dessert. Children that have good table manners might be taken out to a restaurant with the rest of the family. But learning to follow a rule is not the same thing as adopting the rule as a belief; knowing the rule is not the same thing as choosing to live by it. Reward and punishment can teach a rule, but something else is required for the child to adopt the rule as a guide for their behavior. Belief in the rule is greater than just complying with it to avoid missing dessert. It is also important to note that rewards and punishments serve a different purpose for children than they do for adults. An adult might be arrested and put in jail for stealing. The law against stealing exists to protect other people from thieves, not just to teach people not to steal. Rules, or laws, for adults have a societal purpose while rules for children are based on teaching them to become members of a social order—to be good citizens. Society does not work very well when laws are the sole determinant of moral order. In fact, society fails if people openly steal whenever they think they will not be caught. So this discussion of rules and rewards is about how children learn and civil society depends on this learning process. Laws exist as a failsafe when this learning process in childhood has failed.

Community and Belonging

Children learn in the context of family and school. When this is not possible, they learn from caregivers and other adult role models. This learning entails more than acquiring factual knowledge; it also includes learning the moral values or beliefs on which they will live their lives. So moral learning, the learning of beliefs about right and wrong, is a critical foundation for society. This works in part because people are social creatures and belonging to a social group is somehow essential to becoming a successful adult. Thus the role of parents and caregivers in teaching a system of moral beliefs exists in a social framework that either supports or undermines these efforts. When the school, church, or community group projects beliefs that parallel those of the parents, learning is reinforced. Learning becomes much more difficult when these belief systems conflict.

As children grow, enter school, and take part in community activities, they are also exposed to an expanding circle of belief systems. This can conflict with what they have learned from their parents, but it can also enrich their own moral foundation. Communities are more diverse than families and this diversity leads to questioning as the child grows. This reaches a tipping point in adolescence.

Adolescence: Breaking from Parents

Adolescence is often a painful process for everyone in the family. This is most immediately apparent to the adolescent, but it soon affects siblings and parents as well. Often this starts with a foreboding sense of disquiet as the adolescent begins to question cherished beliefs. When adolescents feel that their questions are not respected, they often turn to their peers. Having spent their entire lives listening to their parents and accepting their parents' beliefs, adolescents now begin to question everything. This, in turn, can feel like a betrayal of the family to parents and sometimes to siblings. But a child cannot become an adult unless they come to terms with deciding for themselves what they will and will not believe. Questions of right and wrong now require much more than the recitation of rules as an answer and the adolescent often finds answers to these questions from adults to be unsatisfactory. They want to know why. What was a black-and-white guide to right and wrong becomes a confusing shade of gray. Becoming an adult means choosing your own beliefs and this means asking hard questions. What is the proof that a given belief is best? Although knowledge can be proven with evidence, this is not the way beliefs work. If these questions about beliefs are never asked, they can never be answered, but that does not make this process easy for anyone.

Thus, the role of parents with adolescents changes dramatically. Rules must be tempered with reasons and parental authority must be reframed. In the absence of factual proof, parents can offer personal testimony to support the changing beliefs of adolescents. Parents worry that the growing child will make bad choices and try to protect the adolescent from these choices. But making bad choices is a necessary part of growing up. Just as parents are not infallible, it is a sure thing that their children will not become infallible adults. The trick here is to help the adolescent keep bad choices to a minimum and learn important lessons from each choice. In the absence of the freedom to make such choices, the adolescent cannot become an independent adult.

Is Childhood Faith an Advantage or Disadvantage?

With all of the turmoil and uncertainty of adolescence, it might be tempting to wonder if beliefs formed in childhood are really good things. If you do not have a foundation of beliefs from your parents, there is less to rebel against in your teenage years. Having experienced the questioning of beliefs, one might think that childhood beliefs are just biases to be overcome. Conflict with parents and other role models about new beliefs in an adolescent might lead to a lifetime of estrangement. People can spend their whole lives trying not to be their parents and this can spill over to problems in the next generation as well. Nevertheless, it is hard to imagine that dealing with important questions would be any easier in the absence of a belief system derived from family and community in childhood. In fact, developing a faith in childhood affords a powerful advantage. Learning about faith gives children a head start on how to think about such things as they grow up. Beliefs are contextual (see chapter 3) and learning in childhood provides such a context. Ideally, children can learn the moral reasons behind the rules they are taught to follow and this can, in turn, lead to a stronger foundation for adult beliefs. Perhaps it is true that the beliefs of children are not necessary for them to form sound values as adults, but that does not mean they are not helpful to the process. The faith of children must be questioned in adolescence, but these questions are answered with affirmation later in life more often than not. So now, we need to consider how faith takes place in an adult who is fully free and capable of reaching his or her own conclusions.

2

Adult Faith

Much has been written about childhood development. Entire areas of study are devoted to how children learn language, develop motor skills like walking, and grow intellectually by learning to read and write. Reading the child development literature might lead one to think that development ends at age eighteen and that adulthood is somehow a static state. But this is not the case. We now know that brain development continues to occur throughout life and that college students think differently about problems than adults in mid-life. The world of a young adult is filled with potential and with dreams and fears for the future while the elderly often live in a world of memories with dreams and regrets about the past. Human development does not end with adulthood but is a continuous process of learning and changing from birth to death. This is true for both intellectual and moral growth; what we know and what we believe evolve over time. So we should consider adult faith to be a journey and not a destination.

The faith of children starts with beliefs they learn from adults and is tempered by what they learn in school and by their own experiences. Beliefs are tested and adapted during adolescence, but this testing is a bit like learning to walk on a high wire while using a net. Adolescents have adults in their lives to help them recover from mistakes and society takes a more tolerant attitude toward mistakes by adolescents that it does with adults. In adulthood, the safety net is removed when society judges our behavior. But here we reach a crucial point: it is *behavior* that is judged, not belief. Even if we believe that stealing is not wrong, we are still punished only if we are caught stealing because society can judge only how we act. So even though beliefs guide behavior, society acts as though it is our behavior that reveals our beliefs. This raises a profound question. If we claim to believe in something but do not act accordingly when faced with life decisions, do we really believe it? Is faith something we can simply profess, or must it be demonstrated by action? Struggling with this question moves us far beyond the faith of children.

Belief and Behavior

> "To believe in something, and not to live it, is dishonest."—Mahatma Gandhi[1]

Our lives are determined by circumstances and choices, by what happens to us and by what we decide to do. It is useful to consider how differently people weigh these two factors. If you think your life is mostly determined by what happens outside of you, you have adopted what psychologists call an external locus of control. If you instead think of life as a set of choices you make, you have an internal locus of control. It is probably true that we all have a balance of these two perspectives, but the degree to which we favor one over the other has a lot to do with how we live our lives. People with strong belief systems are more likely to see life circumstances as a series of tests to their beliefs. For example, if you have a strong belief in democracy as a form of government, you might have to reconsider this belief if democracy fails to produce justice. Your belief has to be tempered by your experience. Democracy is

1. Goodreads, Belief Quotes.

not perfect. Maybe it is our job to work to make it more perfect if we truly believe in it. Circumstances cannot be controlled, but choices and actions can. Without a strong system of beliefs, there is little to guide choices anyway, so circumstances might hold greater sway. But even people with a strong faith system can still be overwhelmed by the vicissitudes of life, particularly when circumstances go badly.

Regardless of where you might fall on the continuum between internal and external locus of control, you have to come to terms with connecting belief and behavior. When our behavior consistently matches our values, we have *integrity*. Inconsistency between what we claim to believe and the choices we make creates dissonance and this disconnect should cause us to either reconsider the belief or modify the behavior. If we believe in helping others, but habitually fail to do so, the resulting lack of integrity undermines the truth of our belief. Thus, adults have opportunities daily to demonstrate integrity, or not. We exist in the real world and our beliefs only hold up if we actually live by them.

If life circumstances present us with choices and if our choices should be based on our beliefs, then our beliefs need to be clear and our convictions strong. Adult faith is a daily tool to guide these choices and the tests can range from simple to profound. So it matters if we have beliefs, it matters how strongly we hold them, and it matters if our choices reflect integrity with these beliefs. Having adult beliefs starts with four basic questions that cannot easily be addressed until adulthood: Am I better off with beliefs than without them? How do beliefs change over time? Should I share my beliefs with others? And what should I do when it is costly to live in accordance with my beliefs?

Am I Better Off with Beliefs than Without Them?

> "Every mental act is composed of doubt and belief, but it is belief that is the positive, it is belief that sustains thought and holds the world together."—Søren Kierkegaard[2]

Philosophers have coined the term *moral nihilism* for the lack of belief in any particular ideal of good. That this has been studied and discussed by learned people suggests that it should not be dismissed without consideration. One could certainly argue that having beliefs means we are limited to actions that do not violate these beliefs. On the surface of things, the freedom to do whatever we want whenever we want might seem appealing. This is less rare in the world than one might think. Our society is based on rules such as a rule that stealing is bad, so we have laws against stealing from others. Most of us would even claim that we *believe* stealing is wrong. And yet we commonly see looting taking place after natural disasters or during riots. Is stealing still wrong if we know we will not be caught and cannot be punished? Perhaps the laws against stealing are in place only to keep poor people from appropriating the property of rich people. We even have stories from literature that justify stealing under some circumstances. Consider the story of Robin Hood for instance. Does the local ruler being a corrupt tyrant justify Robin Hood's stealing his property and giving it to the poor? Is his stealing equally justified if Robin Hood keeps the spoils? Is it equally justified if he steals from people other than the ruler? If there are really exceptions, maybe it makes no sense to believe that stealing is wrong. Does a belief that stealing is wrong mean that it is always wrong?

Most people who have studied moral nihilism find that it contains an inherent contradiction that violates the rules of logic. If I choose to have no beliefs because beliefs only restrict my freedom, then I believe in freedom and consider my freedom to be more important than social rules. But a belief in complete freedom

2. Goodreads, Belief Quotes.

of action is itself a belief. Are moral nihilists really moral nihilists or do they just have beliefs that fall outside of the social mainstream? Another argument against moral nihilism is that it tends to turn out badly. People who steal often get caught and are then exposed to societal punishment. This punishment might result in legal charges and imprisonment or in social estrangement and isolation. Do I really want to live next door to someone who has no problem with stealing from me if given the chance? So moral nihilism seems to fail logically and it seems to fail from a utilitarian point of view; it results in unpleasant outcomes. However inconvenient beliefs might be, it is probably impossible to have no beliefs at all.

Perhaps one might argue that beliefs do not matter in a social sense; only behavior matters. As long as we do not steal, does it really matter whether or not we believe it is wrong? The problem with this point of view is that never stealing might be considered the same thing as having a belief that one should not steal. Similarly, perhaps one can believe stealing is wrong, but still steal under some circumstances. It is hard to make sense of a stated belief when it is disconnected from behavior. So any serious consideration of moral nihilism tends to lead us back to the idea that our lives are safer and more successful when we acknowledge our beliefs about right and wrong.

How Do Beliefs Change Over Time?

Our beliefs would not be worth much if they changed with the weather. On the other hand, extreme inflexibility of belief can be dangerous both for individuals and for society. We have already learned that beliefs cannot be proven, but they also should not be considered a belief if they are provably false. So we are confronted with a problem when considering the story of Robin Hood. If we believe that stealing is always wrong, then Robin Hood is a villain and not a hero. This is one way to interpret the story. Another approach is to modify our belief that stealing is always wrong to a belief that it is usually, but not always wrong—to make this belief conditional. The ability to modify beliefs based on condition is a characteristic of adult faith. Beliefs need to be tested in the real world and the ability to learn and adapt is essential. But how do we know the difference between modifying or improving a belief and simply rationalizing when we violate it? As it turns out, the story of Robin Hood offers us a good example. Two adults might read this story and reach different conclusions about his goodness or lack thereof. This is why the story is valuable. We can talk about it with others in a way that is less threatening than talking about our own choices in life; so the story endures. It allows us to think about the question of stealing from either an absolute or a relative perspective thereby learning about the boundaries of our belief that stealing is wrong.

It is not a bad thing when our beliefs change; it is a sign of moral health. But that does not mean that belief can be so situational that there is no real belief in the first place. There needs to be a middle ground between unlimited flexibility, sometimes called moral relativism, and excessive rigidity of belief, sometimes called moral absolutism. Finding this middle ground in our own conduct and in our relationships with others is an essential characteristic of adult faith. This will be discussed in more detail in chapters 6 and 7.

Should I Share My Beliefs with Others?

A clear sense of our own values and purpose might be necessary for successful adult life, but they are not sufficient. We are not alone in the world and our success and happiness depends on how we interact with other people. This means that we need a code of behavior that fits into our community and society and this code of behavior must balance conformity and individuality. Children are taught to share toys, to follow instructions, and to respect others, but these are rules. Will these rules be adopted in adulthood or will they be changed or ignored entirely? If we believe in sharing with others, how should we respond when others do not share with us? Becoming an adult means confronting injustice, but this is just another way of saying that we need to confront behavior from others that does not conform to our own beliefs. We might have been taught to respect others, but what happens when we encounter behavior not worthy of respect? Is it possible to respect people while not respecting what they do?

The most important interactions we have with others take place within our families and communities. In adulthood, we might choose a life partner and start a family of our own. This requires a compromise between two sets of family values. The values formed in two separate families will never be exactly the same. In modern society, we are also likely to encounter people with very different values in the community. Learning to compromise with family, friends, and co-workers is critical to social harmony. But how much compromise is enough? Are there things we cannot or should not compromise? Strength can come from these differences, but so can conflict. Compromise can occur only when we openly discuss differences. Our beliefs guide our own behavior, but they also form our expectations about those around us.

This creates a series of problems. First, can we share our values without judging the values of others? What is the difference between judging others and judging their values? Second, can we find ways to live with people who will not accept our beliefs? Can we learn how to talk about our beliefs in ways that enhance relationships rather than damaging them? Finally, can we defend our beliefs when they are questioned or will we simply get angry and withdraw from these interactions? No matter how challenging these problems might be, it is hard to argue that never talking about our beliefs would be a better alternative. Discussions about beliefs are one way for us to know when our own beliefs need to be amended. Such discussions also help us to better understand the other people in our lives. So, in many ways, discussing beliefs is essential to healthy human relationships.

What Happens When Beliefs Are Costly?

> "You never know how much you really believe anything
> until its truth or falsehood becomes a matter of life and
> death to you."—C.S. Lewis[3]

Even if we have a strong sense of our own beliefs and a good grasp on how to interact with others, there is still the matter of conviction to consider. Some of our choices have little consequences, but others will change the course of our lives. Are our values strong enough to be tested? How can we know which belief is more important when there is a conflict between two of them? For example, most people would agree that killing is wrong, but is it ever acceptable to take a life in order to save another? If we believe that social order is important, is there ever a time when we should take a stand that is different from the social authorities or norms around us? One approach to managing costly beliefs is to avoid them. We always have the option of keeping our beliefs to ourselves, thereby avoiding difficult choices. This is called living in *moral isolation*. Another option is to make sure all of our beliefs are conditional enough that we can easily excuse ourselves from not following them. This is called *moral relativism*. But sooner or later, anyone who believes in justice and kindness will be confronted with choices about how to deal with injustice and cruelty.

Strong beliefs are like strong steel; they must be flame tempered in the real world around us. So it is useful to consider those times when our beliefs make us unpopular or even unsafe. There clearly can be significant risks from standing strong in our beliefs. On the one hand, one might argue that there is nothing worth dying for, but if this is our approach, how can we explain others choosing to die for something they believe? Are they foolish or are they virtuous? Courage can be defined as acting on one's beliefs despite danger or disapproval. Most people value safety, but they also value courage. Courageous people are not without fear; they overcome fear. Perhaps we could say they are more afraid of violating their beliefs than they are of the consequences of following

3. Goodreads, Belief Quotes.

them. We could also say that fear and risk are needed to truly test our beliefs. People who seek danger unnecessarily are reckless, but people who always avoid danger have a hard time making the world around them a better place. When should we retreat to fight another day? When should we reconsider the beliefs that place us at risk? And when should we take a stand? If we choose to take a stand, what are our motives? Maybe we are seeking the respect of others. Maybe we are seeking self-respect. Maybe we are listening to a higher calling about those things that matter most in our lives. In any case, we need to learn more about the strength of our beliefs and the conflicts that occur when life presents us with moral choices. Fortunately, there are ways to learn about these choices. If we have religious faith, we might consult Scripture or prayer. This will be discussed later. Even without religious faith, we can study the choices made by others and we can consult with people we respect.

Finding History in the Search

In 1543 shortly before his death, Nicholaus Copernicus published a book espousing a new scientific theory that the earth and other planets orbited the sun. This theory was based on his astronomical observations and on his research of ancient Greek writings. He dedicated the book to Pope Paul III.[4] Within two years of its publication, the book came under criticism from both Catholic and Protestant church leaders as a heretical contradiction of the widely held notion that the earth was at the center of the universe. Ninety years later, Galileo Galilei was charged with heresy by the Inquisition and placed under house arrest for the rest of his life after he openly supported Copernicus's theory. Galileo had previously published papers about the moons of Jupiter, the phases of Venus, and the source of the ocean tides.[5] By that time, the geocentric view of the solar system was largely discredited in the scientific

4. Danielson, *The Book of the Cosmos*, 104.
5. Danielson, *The Book of the Cosmos*, 145.

world. Galileo did not challenge the church with regards to theology, only arguing in terms of mathematical and astronomical data. He was given every opportunity to recant his position during his trial, but he refused to do so even though his life and liberty were clearly in jeopardy. He was an old man at the time of his trial and was already famous as a scientist, one of the most important scientists of his or any era. But he stood his ground nonetheless. When this story is told in history class, it is usually framed as a choice between the beliefs of church leaders and those of Galileo. The church leaders certainly believed that the earth was at the center of the solar system. But Galileo did not *believe* in Copernicus's model, he *knew* it to be true. Galileo had evidence based on observation and experiment for the heliocentric model. The belief on which Galileo took a stand was a belief in the scientific method. In essence, he believed that beliefs must be changed when there is conclusive proof that they are false and that scientific evidence constituted such proof. For this reason, many people consider him to be the father of modern experimental science. To consider the geocentric and heliocentric models to be two competing beliefs is to mischaracterize them both. By the time of Galileo, the geocentric model was a disproven theory and the heliocentric model was proven knowledge based on evidence. Thus began a tension between religion and science that continues to this day.

On July 4, 1776, fifty-six members of the American Continental Congress signed the Declaration of Independence.[6] They signed the document to declare American independence from England and in doing so made an historic statement of values. In its preamble, they declared their belief in "self-evident truths," that all men are created equal and endowed by their creator with unalienable rights. They declared that they were opposed to government that was not based on the consent of the governed. At the time the declaration was written, it was a clear act of treason. All fifty-six signed the document knowing they might be hanged. The circumstances of the time offered little reason to believe that a war with England would turn out well for the thirteen poorly organized

6. Middlekauff, *The Glorious Cause*, 312.

American colonies. And yet, each of them signed the document. With the hindsight of history, we consider the signers of the declaration to be heroes. The images of some of them are enshrined on monuments and on our currency. Cities and states are named after them. Their fame is based not just on their courage, but, more important, on the vision created by their statement of belief. They made no effort to prove these beliefs; they considered them self-evident. In doing so, they galvanized a new nation around these values. Would their courage have been less impressive or the ideas less important if the American Revolution had failed? Given the risk, how many of us would have signed the Declaration of Independence even though few of us would argue against these unalienable rights? The idea that government should be subject to the consent of the governed was a pretty radical idea in 1776. It was an untested belief. That is why people refer to the American model of government as an experiment in democracy. The successes of this form of government are obvious to us now. Most of us would say that we know that democracy is the preferred form of government, at least for our own country. Is democracy a proven system? Probably yes. Would everyone in the world agree with this? Definitely not. American society is still far from realizing the full extent of these values. We might believe that all men are created equal, but does our country really live with integrity regarding this belief? The signers of the Declaration of Independence set a very high bar for us—a bar we still struggle to reach. But many of them owned slaves, a behavior very hard to reconcile with their stated beliefs. Our country still struggles with this contradiction.

In 1933, Adolph Hitler became chancellor of Germany and soon thereafter began to build a society based on a goal of ethnic purity. Believing that social and ethnic pluralism were sources of weakness, the Nazi regime imprisoned and killed millions of people over the ensuing twelve years, a slaughter that was stopped only at the end of the Second World War. Opposition to this movement was dealt with harshly.[7] Today, outside of the Reichstag in Berlin, there is a small and rather inconspicuous memorial to

7. Gil, *An Honorable Defeat.*

the ninety-six German political leaders who opposed Hitler. The memorial lists their names and the dates and locations of their imprisonment and death in concentration camps. Later in 1942, a poorly organized resistance movement called the White Rose openly opposed Hitler leading to the arrest and execution of the five student leaders of the group. Perhaps the most famous resister of Nazi values within Germany was Dietrich Bonhoeffer, a German minister and theologian. In 1933, Bonhoeffer refused a post as parish minister in Berlin in protest of Nazi policies and instead took a position at two German-speaking churches in London. But Bonfoeffer ultimately did not flee Germany to avoid the Nazis. He continued to speak out against them and started a seminary for the study of non-violent resistance. He traveled throughout England and visited the United States to raise money to support the seminary and other church activities in Germany. While there, he wrote a famous letter to his friend and colleague Reinhold Niebuhr in which he stated, "I must live through this difficult period in our national history with the people of Germany. I will have no right to participate in the reconstruction of Christian life in Germany after the war if I do not share the trials of this time with my people."[8] Bonhoeffer returned to Germany on the last sailing ship to cross the Atlantic before America entered the war. In 1943, he was imprisoned at the age of thirty-six. In 1945, near the end of the war, Bonhoeffer was hanged by the Gestapo. His books *The Cost of Discipleship* and *Letters and Papers from Prison* are testaments to the strength of his beliefs and his willingness to stand firm when they were challenged.[9] Were these German men and women less heroic and noble than the American colonists who signed the Declaration of Independence? Were they foolish? Nearly every one of them died for their beliefs and few of their names are widely known today.

History is full of examples of people who did or did not stand up for their beliefs in the face of dangerous opposition. Hearing or reading about these stories can help us to understand the very

8. Robertson, *Dietrich Bonhoeffer: Selected Writings*, 102.
9. Bonhoeffer, *The Cost of Discipleship*.

real struggles they were undergoing at the time of their choices. From this history, one can find examples of courage and cowardice, strength and weakness. Some of these people are remembered as heroes and others are mostly forgotten. There were plenty of leaders in the American colonies who remained loyal to English rule. Were they wrong? Other famous people fled from Nazi Germany rather than staying to oppose Nazism. Were they smarter than Bonhoeffer or were they just pursuing a different destiny? Too often history is taught as a series of dates and events to be remembered, but a deeper approach to history can instruct us about the choices of others as we learn to make our own.

Finding Others in the Search

"Believing everyone is dangerous, but believing nobody is more dangerous."—Abraham Lincoln[10]

When we are faced with a moral choice in our lives, few of us head to the library or the internet to find stories about dead people we've never met. The religious among us might consult Scripture or talk with clergy. We also might talk with loved ones, friends, or co-workers. But if our beliefs are our own, what is the point of asking other people? Aren't our beliefs and choices ours and ours alone? Consulting with others in our lives is almost universal in making important choices about how and when to act on our beliefs. Clearly there is more at work here than just our social natures as human beings. In fact, it is often hard to know if we accurately understand our circumstances and it can be even harder to know ourselves well enough to recognize problems with our assumptions and motives. So, the two main reasons for consulting others are to confirm our understanding of the situation and to confirm our understanding of ourselves.

Complex moral choices are dependent on our perceptions about the circumstances surrounding those choices. Suppose we are asked to sign a petition about a problem in our community.

10. Goodreads, Belief Quotes.

How well do we understand the problem? Do we have an accurate understanding of the beliefs of those proposing the petition and of those opposing it? Have we carefully considered all facets of the problem? Asking those around us can help to clarify our own misconceptions about the issue and proposed solutions. But whom should we ask? Clearly we would want to talk with people we trust. We should also want to talk with people who know about the issue. We might want to talk with people who agree with us, but if we are smart, we should also talk with people who disagree. We cannot learn much from those who agree with us all the time. Sometimes it might seem intimidating to talk with those who see things differently. Perhaps doing so might undermine our beliefs. But then again, maybe that is the point. If our beliefs are strong, they can hold up under scrutiny. If our beliefs are weak, maybe they need to change.

It is also critical to talk with people who know us well. Ultimately, to be true to ourselves means we need to know ourselves, and sometimes this is a real challenge in testing times. Maybe our opinions about a given issue are clouded by our opinions of those on one side or the other of the argument. Just because we do not like someone does not mean they are not right. So friends and family members can help us to stay true to ourselves in making important choices. We do not need to face the world alone. Just as we need to be open to the ideas of others, we need to understand the limitations of our own knowledge and the potential inconsistencies in our system of beliefs.

Finding Yourself

Children are often asked what they want to be when they grow up. Their answers can range from amusing to inspiring, but in early adulthood this question becomes serious. What sort of work do I want to do? What should I study in college? What kind of person do I want to be? Young adults might be consciously aware of these questions, or not. They might be anxious to find answers or they might resist taking the questions seriously. But sooner or later, they either make choices or the world forces choices on them. Even unemployed high school dropouts who live with their parents have made a choice, perhaps by refusing to choose. Some questions are hard to escape. Why am I here? What sort of person do I want to be? Central to answering these questions is a process of adopting beliefs about life and the most basic of these beliefs has to do with identity. Is this identity pre-destined, or is it a choice? Do I have control of this decision? How much do I care about what other people think? How much do I want to be like those around me and how much do I want to be different? Some of the answers might come from emulating those we respect. Others come from trying to be different from those we revile. Some of the answers come through planning and others are best answered by trial and error. Self-confidence means being comfortable in one's own skin and this, in turn, requires a strong sense of self. So identity and purpose are goals to be strived for in adulthood, even though they might never be perfectly attained.

Our most important life choices are hard to make if the first time we think about values is when such a choice needs to be made. One of the central purposes of education is to inform us about the world, but a purpose less talked about is to learn who we are. In most languages of the world, the verbs "to be" and "to do" are among the most common. We tend to be judged by our actions, our successes and our failures. But what we do follows from who we are and this is built around what we do and do not believe. Here then is the challenge: how much thought and reflection has gone into our sense of self? Are there things we can do to build a strong system of values, a system strong enough to depend on in tough times? To answer this question, we will need to know far more about the process of believing in something. This, in turn requires us to go back to the basics.

PART II

Fundamental Questions

3

What Does It Mean to Believe?

In the previous chapters, we have discussed how beliefs develop
and how they relate to behavior. It is now time to delve more
deeply into what it actually means to believe something. The best
way to begin is to state clearly what believing is not. First, believing something is not the same as knowing it. Knowing requires
evidence and proof; belief does not. Knowing something requires
it to be provably true. Believing something does not require proof
of truth but does require an absence of provable falsehood. In both
knowing and believing, there is the possibility of error. For centuries, human beings "knew" that the world was flat. They based
this on the self-evident appearance of the world around them and
on the fact that other people claimed to know the same thing. The
world was considered flat because it looked flat and because everyone else thought so too. Even though the ancient Greeks found
evidence that the world was a sphere, it was not accepted as truly
spherical until much later. Nearly everyone now considers the flat
world model to be false and we all "know" that the world is spherical. Similarly, beliefs once held to be true can be proven false.
Some people have chosen to "believe" that the world would end

on a specific day only to find that this did not occur as predicted. Once the belief was demonstrated to be false, it ceased to be a true belief and is now considered an error or even a delusion.

Second, beliefs are not simply social rules. Human beings are social creatures and nearly all of us live in the presence of other people. Within our social environments, there are rules of behavior—social rules established within the group to guide the behavior of its members. Examples might include the rules of common courtesy, rules about personal space, and rules about property. In most societies, there is a social convention that people should wear clothes when in public. Those who violate this rule might be ostracized or even arrested. Like beliefs, these rules guide behavior for those within the social group, but they are rules and not beliefs. Social conventions might be formalized into laws such as a law that prohibits stealing things that belong to other people. One can follow these rules without believing in them. Belief is an internal process by which one adopts a value for reasons that go beyond social convention.

Third, believing something is not the same thing as having an opinion or judgment about it. Judgments and opinions do not necessarily lead to action and beliefs generally do. We might have an opinion that rock music is too loud, but continue to listen to rock music anyway. If that opinion was a belief, we would generally not listen to rock music at all or we would only listen to it with the volume turned down or with ear protection. So our perceptions about the world start as just thoughts or sensory input and we then use a mental model to form judgments about our perceptions. If our judgment is that the perception is true and that demonstrable proof exists that it is true, then we might say we know something that we did not know before. If the judgment cannot be proven true, but we choose to assume it is true and make decisions accordingly, we have established a belief.

So one way to begin to understand belief is to understand its boundaries. But the boundaries between judgment and belief and between belief and knowledge can be very difficult to define in a way that makes sense from one person to the next. Some people require a lot of evidence before deciding that a judgment is knowledge and other are convinced by less rigorous evidence. Thus reasonable people can disagree about whether such a judgment qualifies as knowledge. Similarly, people can require different degrees of certainty before adopting a judgment as a belief and taking action on it. Some people are stubborn about sticking to their beliefs while others are easily convinced to change beliefs on the basis of new information. So these boundaries are hard to pin down. Some people insist on very strong proof while others are easier to persuade with the same amount of evidence.

Perceptions, Judgments, Opinions, and Belief

In everyday language, we often consider the following sentences to mean the same thing:

a. I think it is going to rain today.
b. I believe it is going to rain today.

The first sentence states an opinion or judgment. The second sentence offers a belief. This distinction was discussed earlier when we defined these terms. Most people would make no distinction between these two statements. Some people might be confused if someone believed it was going to rain, but did not take an umbrella when leaving the house. But the difference is subtle. What about the following two sentences?

a. I think God exists.
b. I believe God exists.

Now the difference seems more important. The first sentence seems weak compared to the second, as though we are hedging our bet. The second sentence seems to carry some obligation with it. There is not much emotional attachment required to make the first statement. The second statement seems to have more commitment and gravitas. If we believe God exists, we should be able to explain how we act accordingly even if we cannot provide proof to convince the skeptical listener. Imagine how the two sentences might be continued:

a. I think God exists, but I am not sure. I can't prove it. I do not know for sure, but a lot of people I respect seem to be convinced.

b. I believe God exists. I may not be able to prove it to you, but my life is guided by my faith.

So in some contexts, opinions and beliefs seem pretty similar, but in other cases, they seem quite different. Of course the difference is less apparent if the person making the statement has a very loose connection between their beliefs and their behavior. Perhaps a person might say she believes God exists but makes no effort to behave any differently than the person who just thinks so. Maybe some with this belief don't even act differently than the person who believes God does not exist. This highlights the problem with trying to explain the difference between belief and opinion. On the one hand, we might argue that if our behavior is the same whether or not we believe in God, then we must not really believe it. On the other hand, few of us behave with perfect integrity about the things we believe. Do people without integrity between their beliefs and actions really hold the beliefs they claim? How can we know when beliefs are genuine?

The answer, of course, is that we cannot know. This is why it is worth our time to seriously think about what we mean when we say we believe something. Belief brings with it an obligation to behave in accordance with the belief. For some people, it means a lot to believe something. For others, the connection between belief and behavior is less strong. To ask how we can know whether someone actually believes something raises the question of how we can know anything. That brings us to the boundary between knowledge and belief, which will be discussed below.

Belief and Social Convention

Just as it is not always easy to understand the boundary between judgments and belief, it is also not always clear how to distinguish belief from social convention. When we discussed how children learn table manners, we talked about the rule learned from our parents that throwing food at the table is unacceptable. Children learn this rule as well as hundreds of other rules about how to act in accordance with the rules of the society in which they live. Some of these rules become internalized as beliefs. Others we simply follow to avoid punishment or to show respect for social convention. The difference might be impossible to distinguish by the outside observer because behavior in both cases complies with the rule. The difference might become more apparent if the behavior continues when no one is watching or when the person being observed is in a setting where others throw their food. While this distinction might seem trivial, beliefs are more than social mores. One can follow social mores without believing in them. One can also believe that social mores are wrong and violate them as an act of protest. But in many circumstances, complying with a rule can be hard to tell from believing in it.

Theories of Knowledge

The study of how we come to know things is called epistemology, an area of study within philosophy.[1,2] For centuries, philosophers have studied this topic and there are dozens of models by which we might understand knowledge. While it is beyond the scope of this book to review this broad field, we need to have a clear understanding of what knowing means if we are to understand its boundary with believing.

Epistemology dates back to at least the ancient Greeks and is an area of study to which scholars have devoted their lives. The central question in this field is to understand what it means

1. Nagel, *Knowledge: A Very Short Introduction.*
2. Moser, *The Oxford Handbook of Epistemology.*

to know something. This question then leads to scores of others. Does objective truth exist in the world beyond our ability to know it, or is truth just a model in our heads? Is there really a difference between believing something and knowing it; can we really "know" anything? If knowledge requires evidence, what sort of evidence is sufficient? Is knowledge a social convention or is it independent of social context? If evidence comes from our five senses, are our senses reliable? If evidence can come from the testimony of others, how can we know if their testimony is reliable? If we use logic to prove something, can we trust the logic of our own minds? Do we need to be 100 percent sure to say we know something, or will something less than 100 percent suffice? Does the level of required certainty vary from one case to the next? Different philosophical theories would offer different answers to these questions and our purpose here is not to review them all. So we will start with answers that are generally agreed upon.

First, most philosophers agree that an external world exists and that truth exists in this external world. Further, they tend to agree that we have the capacity to know things about the external world. The school of philosophy that does not accept an external truth or that argues that we cannot know anything about it is called *skepticism*. Skepticism is not easy to refute conclusively, but most serious epistemologists accept external truth. Second, most philosophers agree that knowledge does not exist unless someone knows it. Facts can be true, but they require someone to know them to qualify as knowledge. The classic example here is a coin that is shaken in a closed box. It might be true that the heads side of the coin is facing up, but if no one knows whether the coin is heads or tails, it is not considered knowledge.

Once we agree that we can know things about an objective external world, philosophers argue that for a piece of information to be knowledge, it must have three characteristics. First, it must be true in the external world. We cannot know things that are provably false. Second, we must think that the information is true. It is not knowledge unless we ourselves are convinced of its truth. Finally, there must be a convincing justification or proof that it is true. Adopting this theory to our understanding of belief, we might say that the second condition must also be present for a belief to exist. In other words, knowledge and belief share the condition that the person holding them thinks they are true. Although a belief cannot be conclusively proven to be true, it does not satisfy the definition of belief if it can be proven false. So a belief must satisfy three conditions:

1. the believer assumes the belief to be true even without proof,

2. the believer makes decisions or acts as though it is true, and

3. the belief can be proven neither true nor false.

We might believe something to be true and later find proof that it is, in fact, true. In this case, a belief can become knowledge. We might also believe something to be true and then find convincing evidence that it is not. In this case, it ceases to be a belief and becomes a disproven idea.

Traditionally, philosophers have tended to view knowledge as being either fundamentally based in abstract ideas that exist in the human mind or fundamentally based in the external world as perceived through our senses. Internal abstract ideas are considered to be characteristics of the intellect such as logical deduction or basic mathematics. Philosophers who take this view are called *rationalists*. Those that believe that knowledge starts with sensations about the world are called *empiricists*. Adapting these ideas to belief raises the question of whether our beliefs arise from our experiences or from an innate sense of right and wrong, beauty and ugliness, good and bad.

Up to this point, we have distinguished between things that are true in an understandable real world and things that are false. This implies certainty about truth, but what happens when we cannot be certain? Since it is hard to be absolutely certain about anything, how certain do we need to be to say we know something? Philosophers might consider this problem in two ways. First, maybe our certainty depends on what other people think is true. We are more likely to accept a proposition as true and to say we know it if everyone else thinks so too. This is particularly important when we share ideas in a community of people. The statements of other people can be part of a body of evidence used to establish knowledge. Second, the level of proof we require might be greater if the stakes of being wrong are high. Let's say that we know that a gun is not loaded. Perhaps we know this because we removed all of the bullets and locked the gun in a safe. We might "know" that the gun is not loaded and we might even share this knowledge with others offering our own testimony as evidence. But what would happen if we were asked to point that gun at a loved one and pull the trigger? We would probably refuse to do this in spite of the fact that we "know" it to be empty of bullets. Do we know the gun is empty or don't we? Few would be willing to accept our testimony as evidence if we refused to "prove it" with our actions. Both of these two points are relevant to our discussion of belief. It is easier to believe things that everyone else believes and it is easier to believe when little is at stake. So both knowledge and belief have a social context and both have a conditional context.

Probability and Context

Over the past hundred years, physicists have learned much about the natural world. While we once had a very clear and concrete idea of matter, energy, space, and time, we now are faced with the overwhelming evidence to support the theories of special and general relativity and the theory of quantum mechanics. Special and general relativity have shown us that space and time are not simple concepts. Time moves differently in different reference frames depending on the relative speeds of the frames. Space somehow bends in the presence of massive objects to create what we perceive as gravity. In quantum mechanics, we now know that matter and energy are two versions of the same thing and that the position and speed of a particle at the sub-atomic level can be understood only in terms of probability. These theories of the physical world have great relevance to what we think we can know absolutely and with certainty. If the physical world is probabilistic, then why isn't knowledge probabilistic? If the cosmos is governed by relativity theory, then why isn't knowledge relative as well? And if we can think of knowing things only in a defined context and with less than perfect certainty, what does this mean about our beliefs? It seems clear that our understanding of belief is closely linked to our understanding of knowledge. Perhaps the boundary between knowing and believing is itself a moving target in a world where uncertainty and context seem to matter more than ever before.

So this brings us back to where we started. Knowledge requires someone to know it. Beliefs require someone to believe them. Both knowledge and belief must be able to stand up to evidence from the real world. Knowledge must be provably true and belief cannot be provably false. The boundary between knowledge and belief lies in the standards of evidence needed to convince others. If we again turn to Euclidean geometry as a guide, knowledge is a provable theorem, while belief is a postulate we assume to be true. Geometry would not exist without its postulates; it is built entirely on these postulates. But there would be no point to geometry if it did not allow a shared standard for proving theorems leading to general agreement about their truth. Geometry is very useful in solving real-world problems, and it requires both postulates and theorems to work. Perhaps knowledge and belief cannot be definitively separated. Perhaps they need one another to make any sense.

4

Types of Belief

Now that we have discussed what beliefs are not, it is time to talk about what they are. We have already established three criteria for a belief. The believer assumes the belief is true in the external world, the believer makes decisions or takes actions based on this assumption, and there is not conclusive proof that the belief is either true or false. To make this easier to understand, it is useful to consider different kinds of beliefs, so we will now delve more deeply into some categories of belief as a way to provide specific examples to consider.

Aesthetic Belief

An aesthetic belief is a belief reflecting our feelings about beauty in the real world. It is a belief and not an opinion because we take action on it. We might believe that pizza is the tastiest food in the world. We enjoy pizza every time we eat it. We habitually order pizza at restaurants when given the chance, so we take action on this belief. We cannot prove to anyone else that pizza is the tastiest food, but they cannot prove to us that it is not. We order pizza because we assume, based on all of the previous times we have ordered pizza, that we will like its taste. So we believe the next pizza will be good because other pizzas have been. In a similar way, we might believe that a rose is the most beautiful flower, that Mozart is the greatest composer of music living or dead, or that taking long walks in a forest will help us to relax. All of these are beliefs, and they all might be classified as aesthetic beliefs because they reflect our preferred actions about what looks, sounds, tastes, smells, or feels good or bad. Aesthetic beliefs are about sensory experiences and the choices we make based on those experiences. They satisfy the criteria of a belief. We assume the next rose we smell will smell good, we make choices to seek out roses when given a choice about flowers, but we cannot prove that roses smell the sweetest to anyone else, and they cannot prove to us that they don't.

Of course we do not necessarily always choose to plant roses in our garden even though we might believe them to be the most beautiful flower. We might also believe in the beauty of a variety of flowers. We do not always order pizza in a restaurant because we also like other foods. So an aesthetic belief is not always an absolute guide to our choices. But it is certainly a relative guide. Now the casual reader might consider aesthetic beliefs to be rather trivial, particularly when compared to moral beliefs about right and wrong or a belief that God exists. Nevertheless, aesthetic beliefs are useful in distinguishing between a belief and an opinion.

There is also a darker side of aesthetic beliefs. Sometimes we develop an aesthetic belief under the influence of marketing or branding of a product. Do we believe Coke is better than Pepsi or that Ford cars are better than Chevrolet because of previous experiences or because product advertising has convinced us that we want to be associated with one rather than the other? Branding is a very powerful force. Advertising a product on television, in magazines, or on the internet is expensive because it works. Evidence supports the notion that our aesthetic beliefs are highly influenced by celebrity endorsements or by the association of specific products with favorable attributes that may have nothing to do with the product itself. Perhaps we are willing to pay more money for Nike shoes because of the association of Nike with athletic success or because our favorite basketball player wears their shoes. Perhaps this preference has little to do with our own experience with athletic shoes or the actual value of the shoes themselves. So aesthetic beliefs help us to understand that beliefs can be formed from influences other than experience or logic. If we believe that Nike shoes are better because a famous athlete wears them, can our moral or religious beliefs be influenced in a similar way? The evidence suggests strongly that they can. How does this change the way we think about beliefs in general?

Prognostic Belief

A prognostic belief is a belief about the future. We have already used the example of believing that it will rain tomorrow and carrying an umbrella because of this belief. This example also seems trivial, so instead let's consider a belief that the world will end on a particular date in the future. Beliefs about the end of the world have formed the basis for doomsday cults for centuries. While this seems silly after the date has passed, it cannot conclusively be proven wrong in any other way than to see what actually happens on the day in question. So until the appointed day, it is a prognostic belief. People have made major life decisions based on doomsday beliefs, and such beliefs have always proven false since the world has not yet ended. Maybe someday, one of these will prove true.

Most successful people have at one time or another considered the idea of delayed gratification. Perhaps I believe that if I work really hard in college and get good grades, I might get into medical school. Or maybe I believe that I can play professional basketball if I practice dribbling and shooting hour after hour and day after day. Delayed gratification means that I am willing to invest a lot of work based on a belief about what might happen in the future. It may not be likely that the desired outcome will happen, but it is even less likely that these things will happen if I don't put in the work to get good grades or perfect my skills on the court. So prognostic beliefs can play an important role in life decisions over many years. If all of that work is done only to realize one particular dream, it can lead to great disappointment if the desired outcome does not happen. On the other hand, maybe one learns critical life skills while pursuing a dream, and maybe these skills lead to unexpected outcomes on a completely different career path. This is why successful people usually have a strong work ethic. They pursue a dream of the future, and the work they invest creates opportunities for them.

People can also have negative prognostic beliefs. Maybe a young adult, seeing the experiences of his or her parents, concludes that it does not matter how hard one works. Maybe they believe that success is beyond their grasp and that their dreams can never come true. In such a circumstance it is not hard to understand why the young adult might consider hard work to be a waste of their time. Positive prognostic beliefs are the foundation of hope. Negative prognostic belief can be a foundation for despair. So it is worth taking some time to think deeply about our beliefs regarding the future. If we are optimistic, where does the optimism come from? If we are hopeless, how did we get that way?

It is axiomatic that the future cannot be known. So there can be no knowledge about the future. Our thoughts about the future can be beliefs or they can just be thoughts. As we get older, we get to see how our prognostic beliefs turn out. This, in turn, guides the next generation of our beliefs about the future. Some people fear being wrong about the future. It can be painful to believe in something that never turns out to happen. Prognostic beliefs can also be so unlikely to actually happen that they seem foolish. How much optimism is too much? Optimism about the future leads to risk taking. Little can be accomplished with no risk at all, but excessive risk taking can cause harm.

Beliefs About People

Human beings are social creatures; we live within communities of other people. As a result, we make judgments every day about the other people in our lives. And sometimes, these judgments become beliefs about these people. Can we depend on the support of our parents? Can we trust our best friend? By what criteria do we make judgments about other people and how strong must these judgments be before we are willing to make decisions based on them? Life can be very lonely if we never learn to trust anyone, but it can be dangerous to be too trusting in our relationships with others.

The ability to form beliefs about people is a major developmental task of childhood and adolescence. We start by learning to trust our parents and other adult role models. If we are unable to learn this lesson, it becomes more difficult to trust friends and co-workers as we get older. Isolated and lonely adults have often learned hard lessons from misplaced trust earlier in life. This is one reason why it is so harmful to violate the trust of children.

Children who learn from experience not to trust their parents are also likely to have a hard time learning to be trustworthy themselves. So it is useful to consider how we make decisions about whom to trust. Learning to trust or to love or to respect others begins with experimentation. We cannot learn to trust someone if we never try it out. We start by trusting our parents and teachers and we learn over time whether or not this trust is warranted. Bad experiences early on teach hard lessons about misplaced trust. We cannot learn this skill if we never trust anyone, but we also cannot learn it if we are burned repeatedly by trusting the wrong people. Among all of the developmental tasks of adolescence, few are as important as learning this skill.

Social Belief and Culture

Earlier, we discussed the differences between belief and social custom and made a distinction between social mores and belief. But there is such a thing as a social belief and such beliefs are essential elements of culture. Sociologists use the term *social mores* to refer to the essential or characteristic customs of a culture. A given community might have social mores about how its members interact with one another. Violating these mores could lead to social isolation or even expulsion from the group. Some group members might internalize these social norms to the point that they consistently behave in accordance with the custom even when they are outside of the social group. This varies from person to person and from one social belief to the next. Social beliefs can relate to a wide range of ideas about issues such as religion, politics, or professional norms. Americans are taught that democracy is the best form of government. Physicians are taught that they must keep patient information confidential and that they must first do no harm. People who are members of a church are taught a set of core beliefs that define members of that church. Social beliefs form defining characteristics of social groups. If we accept none of the beliefs of a particular group, it is hard to remain a member of that group.

To clarify this notion, let's consider an historical example. We have already discussed the courage of those who opposed the Nazi regime in Germany in the 1930s and 1940s, but history tells us that those opposing the Nazis were a small minority. Many historians have been mystified about why so many people in Germany supported or remained silent about the rise of the Nazis. Some have claimed that the German people must not have known what was going on in their own country. This begs the question of what we mean by knowing. It is hard to imagine that the signs of Nazi oppression of ethnic and religious minorities were not clear by the late 1930s. Understanding how this oppression came to be tolerated requires us to come to terms with just how powerful social beliefs can be. It also means that we must acknowledge that our own social beliefs can be manipulated just as our aesthetic beliefs can be. The average German person might have been aware of Nazi oppression, but they still highly valued being German. So even if they did not support the Nazis, they did not oppose actions that many of them were probably troubled by because of the risk of being rejected from German society. There was also real physical risk of being imprisoned or killed for speaking out against what had become a group norm. This is not just an issue with German people. It is a real example of how dangerous social beliefs can be in the wrong hands. The lessons of Nazi Germany are a clear cautionary tale. Speaking out before social norms become widely accepted is critical if we want to prevent dysfunctional social beliefs from forming in the first place. This raises the question of how to tell which social beliefs are beneficial and which are dangerous and ultimately to the question of how we tell good from evil or right from wrong in forming our beliefs.

Moral Belief

When you chose to read this book, your first goal may have been to better understand how to make the "right" choices in living your life. Many of our toughest life choices are about our moral beliefs. A moral belief is a belief about what is right and wrong. If you believe in always telling the truth, or if you believe that telling lies is sometimes justified, you have a moral belief. Just as philosophers have studied what it means to know something, there is a branch of philosophy that deals with understanding right and wrong. This field of study is called moral philosophy or ethics.[1] As with epistemology, some of the greatest minds in history have taken up the goal of defining moral truth. The lack of consensus agreement suggests that this is far from a simple issue. In our discussion about 1930s Germany, we considered how the social beliefs of the German people came to accept behaviors that most of us would consider wrong. But why are they wrong? How can we tell if something happening in our own community is right or wrong? What criteria should we use to decide such things? In general, philosophers have approached moral belief along three broad paths.

The oldest approach to ethics is called *virtue ethics*. Tracing its origins to the work of Aristotle, virtue ethicists would say that right and wrong are not actions but are characteristics of the person taking the action. Thus, the right thing to do is what a virtuous

1. Philosophybasics.com.

person would do in the same circumstance. A virtue ethicist might then argue that a virtuous person is someone who devotes time and energy to defining what these virtues are and incorporating them into his or her character. Aristotle claimed that there are four virtues that rise above all others as most important, which he called "cardinal virtues." These are:

- *Prudence*: The prudent person thinks about problems practically and carefully considers the choices to be made. Prudence means being careful or thoughtful about life choices.

- *Temperance*: The temperate person exercises restraint and self-discipline. They act in moderation, avoid excess, and practice self-control.

- *Courage*: The courageous person adheres to his or her values in the face of risk or danger. Soldiers can display physical courage in battle, but anyone can display moral courage in the face of social pressure or economic risk.

- *Justice*: The just person acts with fairness towards others and makes choices based on considering their impact on all participants.

More recent virtue ethicists have advocated for other virtues, but what all have in common is the notion that our actions are derived from having virtue and that our goal in life is to understand and attain virtues. Critics of virtue ethics might ask how we can know which virtues to study and pursue. Are our choices of virtues based on actual criteria? If they are, then where do these criteria come from and how do we know they are the right ones?

The second broad way of thinking about ethics is called *consequentialism*. In this school of thought, actions are good if they produce good outcomes, and we should try to choose the option that will have the best result. For some, the best result is the one that produces the most pleasure for the person making the choice. For others, the best choice is the one that produces the most happiness for the largest number of people. Other consequentialists might argue that the best choice is the one that most benefits society as a whole or the one that most benefits others. What these approaches have in common is the notion that the outcome of our choice is what determines what is right, not our own virtue or our intentions. Making a correct decision then depends on our ability to anticipate its outcome. The central problem with consequentialism is that it tends to discount intention. Sometimes an action produces a beneficial result by accident. Does that mean the choice was right? Sometimes a well-intended action causes harm anyway. Does this mean the choice was wrong?

The third school of ethical thought is that the rightness or wrongness of an action is determined by the degree to which the action conforms to rules of behavior that constitute our duty. This model of ethics is called *deontology*. Perhaps the most famous deontologist was the eighteenth-century philosopher Immanuel Kant.[2] Kant argued that the right choice is based on following a predetermined set of moral rules that he called the categorical imperative. In his view, the categorical imperative is based on three criteria:

1. All our actions should be based on a willingness to have everyone else take the same action universally. So it is wrong to steal because we would not want everyone in the world to steal.

2. All our actions should treat humanity as an end in itself and not just a means to attain another goal. So it is wrong to lie or to own slaves, because in doing so we manipulate and use other people.

3. Our actions are our own autonomous choices. So we cannot defend immoral choices by saying that others caused us to make them.

More recent deontologists have expanded on these ideas to create other categorical principles or to build on Kant's ideas. All of these theories share the notion that our motives and core beliefs are what

2. Philosophybasics.com.

determine the rightness or wrongness of a choice rather than simply judging decisions by their outcomes. The main problem with this approach is that it can be hard to defend how the categorical principles are arrived at in the first place. Kant tried to defend his categorical imperative by using logic. For example, he might argue that stealing is wrong because we would not want everyone in the world to steal at will. If everyone stole at will, then no one could count on the safety and security of his or her property and society would be in chaos. This might lead one to ask why we care about private property in the first place. Perhaps rules preventing theft are just a way of allowing the weak to be protected from the strong or the foolish to be protected from the clever.

One way to solve the problem of defending particular categorical rules is to simply say that the rules came from God. Thus, some deontologists have advocated for systems of rules coming from religious texts such as the Ten Commandments. They would then argue that it is wrong to steal or to lie because these behaviors are prohibited by the rules handed down by God. Another way to think about this is to accept the Ten Commandments because they have proven to work across the span of history. They work as a moral code of behavior because society functions better when people live by rules that prohibit stealing from or killing others. This, of course, is largely an argument that connects back to consequentialism.

Beliefs about right and wrong somehow seem more important to us than aesthetic or prognostic beliefs. In fact, when we endeavor to talk about beliefs, it is moral beliefs and religion that first come to mind. To some, moral beliefs are simply limits on social behavior. If we accept that it is wrong to lie, our freedom to say whatever we want to say is restricted. This is why some philosophers have viewed morality in general and religion in particular as organized systems of social control by organizations like the state or the church. But all of the schools of ethics would consider lying to be wrong in most situations. Virtue ethicists would argue that lying is wrong because trust in others would be impossible in a society in which everyone lies, so a virtuous person would not lie.

Consequentialists would argue that lying is wrong because others will stop believing us if we lie; the long-term consequences would be adverse. Deontologists would argue that lying is wrong because it violates a basic moral duty of being truthful. But does this mean that lying is always wrong? On this question, the various schools of thought might diverge. Moral beliefs about right and wrong are sometimes codified into social custom. For example, it is not illegal to lie, but it is illegal to lie under oath in a court of law. One way to view such a law is the social incorporation of a moral rule. We restrict a person's freedom to lie in order to protect others from being lied to.

Let's consider some examples as a way to better understand how moral beliefs play out in our lives. Suppose our best friend buys a new dress for a wedding. She then tries on the dress and asks us what we think of it. Further suppose that we really do not like the dress. Should we tell her this? If we tell her the truth, we risk hurting her feelings and asserting our opinion into her personal decision. Maybe we want to protect her from being embarrassed fearing that everyone else at the wedding will think the dress is silly. Maybe we want our friend to trust our honesty or we want to protect our reputation for always telling the truth. We then try to weigh the possible benefits and harms of telling her that we do not like the dress in making our decision about how to answer. This would be a consequentialist approach to the decision. Or we might consider it our duty not to hurt our friend's feeling or our duty never to lie as the foundation for the decision, a deontological approach. In real life, we often try to hedge our bet. We might give an unenthusiastic endorsement of the dress and tell her it is her choice to make. But what if she pushes the question further? How will we respond if she asks us a second time what we "really think"? Now we might be more direct, viewing the follow-up question as permission to be "more honest" with her.

Now imagine a different situation. Suppose our friend has shop-lifted the dress and asks us to tell others we gave it to her. The stakes in this decision are higher. We are being asked to lie to protect an illegal act, and the consequences of our decision are more profound for our friend and for us. In this case, there is a social norm to help us choose. Stealing the dress is illegal, and it might also be illegal to lie to the authorities about it. So the right choice is to refuse to lie, but is it right just because it is illegal or is it morally wrong to lie in this situation regardless of the law? What would a virtuous person do? What is our moral duty? A decision based on moral belief would not use the law as the reason for telling the truth; the decision would be based on a higher principle guiding our behavior. We make the choice to tell the truth based on our conscience. Our conscience tells us that lying is wrong, but where did this notion come from?

One way to simplify all of this is to consider what sort of life we want to live and what sort of reputation we want to build across the span of that life. Few would argue that it is not desirable to be trusted by others and to be able to trust others in return. If we want to be a trusted person, we cannot lie to others. Doing so not only violates the trust of those we lie to, but it also makes others uncertain when we might decide to lie to them. Fundamentally, being trusted means that other people can depend on us to act reliably in a certain way. Our behavior cannot be consistent if we have no moral code about what is right and wrong, but it is our behavior and not our belief that others can see. So our beliefs about right and wrong are understandable to others only on the basis of what we say and do. To be trusted, we must act consistently. To act consistently, we need a set of rules to guide our choices, and we need to act reliably in accordance with those rules. If we want others to trust our word, we cannot lie. Whether we call truthfulness a virtue, value truth-telling because it produces better consequences, or consider truth-telling to be a moral rule, the end result is truthful behavior.

5

Morality and Religious Belief

Over the course of the past one hundred years, it might be fair to say that consequentialist theories of right and wrong have tended to predominate. In part, this is because there is one major problem with both virtue ethics and deontological ethics: it is very hard to defend a list of basic virtues or moral duties. Aristotle defined his cardinal virtues though a process of careful thought and debate. Apparently, Kant defined his categorical imperative through a process of logical deduction. But to many, their choices seem arbitrary. If you don't like their lists, you could simply discount these theories as one way of looking at values. If Aristotle and Kant can pick their core values, then why can't each of us just do the same? Is right and wrong contingent on social agreement? Is right and wrong just a matter of personal choice? A belief that right and wrong vary from person to person and from situation to situation is called *moral relativism*. Taken to the extreme, a moral relativist might argue that there is no objective right and wrong and the search for such core values is doomed to be fruitless. The opposite of moral relativism is *moral absolutism*, which implies that right and wrong are absolute and universal. But for right and wrong to be absolute, we need to know where our core understanding comes from. Philosophers have trouble pinning down a distinction between right and wrong in any way that does not seem a bit arbitrary. So many people look to religion to define core moral values. We can accuse Kant's categorical imperative of being arbitrary, but we may not be so quick to say the same thing about the Ten Commandments or the Quran. Religion allows us to escape the problem of how core values are defined by simply stating that they come from a supernatural power that we cannot fully understand and that these values came into the world before we did. The idea that our understanding of right and wrong comes from God is the realm of religion. So it is hard to have an extended discussion about moral beliefs without eventually encountering religion. Whether or not we think God exists, we will encounter many people in our lives who use religion to guide their choices about right and wrong. Throughout history, religion may be the most frequently used model for moral decision-making; even devout atheists sometimes use the Ten Commandments as a moral guide. Thus, we need to understand religion whether or not we choose to have religious beliefs.

A religious belief is a belief about the existence and nature of God. Those of us raised in religious families are usually taught by our parents that God exists and we are taken to a church or other religious community to be with other people who share the same belief. We are taught that we should learn about God and then follow a set of God's rules as outlined in religious texts like the Jewish Torah, Christian Bible, or the Muslim Quran. So our faith begins with testimony from others and is supported by the social context, literature, and customs of a community. As children, we are taught that the core values of right and wrong are not up to us to define and that these rules are beyond question because they come from God. It is not hard to see how this might cause problems when we encounter people from different religious traditions with a different set of core values. So while philosophy sometimes has a problem with moral relativism, religious teaching can have problems with moral absolutism. Of course this is one of the most frequently cited problems with religion: that it can be inflexible, intolerant, and judgmental.

No matter what we are taught as children, we eventually need to come to terms with deciding about God for ourselves. Religious beliefs are learned in childhood, challenged in adolescence, and adopted or not adopted in adulthood, as are other beliefs. At some point in time, we are confronted with the fact that there is no conclusive proof of God's existence and that the world contains lots of people who don't believe in God or who believe in God in a different way. Somewhat surprisingly, many of those who do not believe in God still believe in following religiously based moral rules such as the Ten Commandments. They still celebrate religious holidays. Some even go to church from time to time. So it is not easy to tell who actually believes what when it comes to religion. If we are not raised in a religious tradition, we might encounter the question of God as adults when we seek answers to deeply important questions about right and wrong or existential questions about why we exist or why the world is the way it is. We might meet someone who shares their religious beliefs with us and seek to learn more about those beliefs. Or we might just encounter people who are using religious reasons for their choices in life and want to know more about why they do so. If you do not believe in God, it can be hard to understand the depth of conviction of those who do. Their beliefs can seem arbitrary and even extreme. For those raised in a religious tradition, it can be equally hard to understand how nonreligious people are able to tell right from wrong. Not being religious does not mean that a person cannot be honest. An atheist can certainly strive for Aristotle's virtues or Kant's categorical imperative. So religious belief might not be necessary for moral behavior. But the atheist seeking a moral code will be faced with the problem of defining why they choose the values they choose, while the religious person can fall back on divine guidance. Of course this can be a real challenge to both groups of people when they encounter each other in a morally complex world. So regardless of which group you might be in, it is useful to better understand religious thought.

Proof of God

> "For those who believe, no proof is necessary. For those who don't believe, no proof is possible."—Stuart Chase[1]

There is no conclusive proof that God exists. There also is no conclusive proof that he does not. The term "conclusive" is used here in the sense of being persuasive to nearly everyone. This has not stopped generations of scholars in religion and philosophy from trying to convince one another. If conclusive proof of God's existence was found, then we would not believe, we would know. Even though religious people seek a relationship with God, they would generally not claim to know him. He is God; he is not completely knowable. Similarly, if there was conclusive proof that God does not exist, then no one could have a genuine belief in him. Recall that our definition of a belief states that the belief cannot be provably false. So let's start our discussion of the evidence with some definitions. A person who believes that one or more God(s) exist is called a *theist*. An *atheist* is a person who believes that God does not exist. An *agnostic* is a person who claims not to know whether God exists. By this definition, we are all agnostics; none of us "know." So a better definition is that an agnostic is a person who does not have a belief about the existence or nonexistence of God. In fact, both theists and atheists have a belief about God, while the agnostic does not.

Over the years, neither the theist nor the atheist has been able to muster a persuasive enough argument for their beliefs about God to be considered knowledge in the eyes of those who disagree with them. But they have certainly tried, so it might help our understanding to consider some of the arguments they have put forth. In general, these arguments have most often been based

1. Goodreads, Belief Quotes.

on the results of believing or not believing in God rather than on direct proof of God's existence.

The atheist's arguments usually take one of four forms. First, they point out all of the harm that has done through the course of history by religious zealotry. It is certainly true that wars have been fought and millions of lives have been lost in religious intolerance between Christians and Muslims, Protestants and Catholics, Hindus and Buddhists, and so on. Many atheists have imagined a world without religion as being better because such conflicts might be avoided. Second, atheists have argued that religion has been used by society to control the behavior of its members thereby restricting the creativity and freedom of individual people. Third, atheists have identified religion as the source of guilt for the religious. Guilt is certainly a source of psychological distress for people when they fail to live up to religious standards. Without such seemingly arbitrary standards, they would have no reason to feel guilty. Fourth, atheists argue that religion stands in the way of human problem solving since religious people can sometimes be seen as obstructing the course of science. An example here might be church's resistance to a heliocentric model of the solar system or to evolution as a biological process. In summary, atheists generally make arguments about the effects of religion in the world to conclude that religious belief is a source of more problems than solutions.

Theists have made arguments that might be summarized along five lines of reasoning. First, a theist sees evidence of the work of God in the majesty of nature and the rules of physics and mathematics. To a theist, it requires a bigger leap of faith to think that everything in the universe is the product of chance than to believe in God as the creator. A second argument is that faith is a source of comfort for people during hard times and theists offer personal testimony and examples from history to support this view. A third argument centers on religious faith as a source of inspiration for works of art and science. Much of the world's great art and music have been inspired by religious themes. Belief in God has also played a role in scientific inquiry. For example, between 1907 and 1915, Albert Einstein searched for solutions to the differential equations that came to define general relativity. He had no a priori guarantee that there were solutions to these equations, and the mathematics was very difficult. But Einstein persisted because of his view of a symmetrical universe built on clear fundamental principles, principles that he felt came from God. His belief helped him to persevere in the face of difficulty. But it also clouded his judgment about quantum mechanics; when he first learned of a quantum atomic model based on probability, he rejected the model, famously stating the he did not believe God played dice with the universe. Einstein was not considered a religious man, but his belief in God as a source of order in the world is everywhere in his work. In a 1930 New York Times interview, Einstein stated:

> I maintain that the cosmic religious feeling is the strongest and noblest motive for scientific research.[2]

Similarly, in his book *The Language of God*, Francis Collins, the leader of the human genome project, links the field of genetics with his belief that understanding genetics leads to an understanding of how God works in nature.[3] A fourth argument made by theists is that ethical models based on belief in God have helped to produce societies throughout history that were built on a shared understanding of morality. Certainly religious faith played a major role in defining the American form of government, which is based on respect for individual rights. One can certainly believe in democracy without believing in God, but the founders of the American republic were, in general, theists. Finally, theists have argued on pure utilitarian grounds that it makes sense to believe in God. The seventeenth-century French mathematician Blaise Pascal is considered to be the father of probability theory. He is also credited with a theist argument called Pascal's wager. Pascal's wager states that either God exists or he does not; if God does not

2. Einstein, *Ideas and Opinions*, 40.
3. Collins, *The Language of God*.

exist, it does not matter whether or not we believe in him; if God does exist, our souls depend on believing. So Pascal argued that it is logical to believe in God because the consequences of being wrong are less severe.

The end result of all of this is that neither the theist nor the atheist can be proven wrong by logical argument, personal testimony, or observable reality. The important point here is that it would not be belief if conclusive proof existed one way or the other. In his famous essay in 1896, *The Will to Believe*, philosopher William James argued that one cannot be proven wrong in deciding to believe or not believe in God.[4] When it comes to provable knowledge, theism and atheism stand on the same footing, the choice to believe or not.

The situation is different when we consider the agnostic. An agnostic is a person without a belief about God one way or the other. Maybe such a person has never thought about it or maybe they simply have chosen not to choose. Perhaps such people require a higher standard of evidence before adopting a belief. Perhaps they fear being wrong and prefer to withhold judgment. So let's consider the ramification of not choosing. If one chooses not to believe one way or the other about God, he or she is left with a need to decide what to believe in instead. Few agnostics are complete nihilists; they nearly always have nonreligious beliefs. Maybe they believe in the scientific method or in American democracy, or in the rule of law. Sooner or later though, like the atheist, they encounter a problem when it comes to moral beliefs. On what basis do they decide about right and wrong? They may be skeptical about religious arguments, but what nonreligious arguments are persuasive to them? Commonly agnostics simply adhere to community standards about right and wrong. They might even cite the Ten Commandments as a reason that stealing or lying or murder is wrong. Maybe their notions of right and wrong, like those of the atheist, are based entirely on consequentialist arguments. For example, agnostics might think killing is wrong because they do not want to be killed and they think society would digress into chaos if

4. James, *The Will to Believe*.

murder and stealing were not prohibited. It also might be the case that agnostics have trouble choosing between the arguments for and against a belief in God because they struggle to understand the arguments. Maybe they think it is safer to remain uncommitted one way or the other since this might make it easier to fit into whichever social group they might be with at the time. An atheist might argue that the agnostic does not choose because they lack the courage to admit their atheism. A theist might argue that not choosing is itself a choice not to believe in God and that there is hardly any practical difference between atheism and agnosticism.

So for centuries, we have stumbled along trying to live with one another amidst this moral confusion. The world is culturally, linguistically, and morally diverse. Some societies try to protect themselves from this diversity by isolating themselves from it. But in an era of global communication, such isolation is hard to maintain. We are all pretty much all free to choose what we will and will not believe, and this is as true for religious beliefs as it is for any other kind of belief. But our choice about belief in God has significant consequences for how we live our lives. If we choose atheism, we need to think through the reasons for all of our other beliefs. If we choose faith in God, we have to explain what sort of God we believe in and how best to understand God's plan for us and for the world we live in.

Choices about God

Perhaps the most significant barrier for the agnostic is the complex questions that arise once one decides to believe in God. There are many different religions in the world and choosing among them is confusing in the best of cases. So it is useful to consider an organized way to think through these choices. The first major question is to decide whether we believe in one or many gods. Some of the world's oldest religions are based on a pantheon of gods representing forces in nature like the sun and moon or areas of human endeavor like war and love. The most prevalent modern religions tend to focus on one God, but some of them consider this God to take several forms. For example, most Christian faiths consider God as a creator, God as a personal savior, and God as a moral guide to be three aspects of a single God. This is similar to the idea that a person can be a man or woman, a husband or wife, a father or mother, and a professional while still being one person. But this still might seem like a belief in three gods not one to believers in Islam or Judaism. From the outside, it is hard to understand why this needs to be so difficult. If there is a single God and this God is impossible to completely understand, then it only makes sense that God might be seen differently from different points of view. If our concept of faith is too complex, we make it hard to achieve. But there are also problems with trying to simplify faith. Efforts to simplify religious faith can easily digress into ideas that lessen God. To a nonbeliever, belief in God can seem quite complicated, but this may be based on a false assumption. People who believe in God do not claim to fully understand him. They have simply chosen to accept God into their lives and work on a daily basis to understand what this means.

A second major challenge is to decide what sort of God one chooses to believe in. The Christian Old Testament, Muslim Quran, and the Jewish Torah describe a God who is majestic, all-knowing, and all-powerful. This God provides us with rules by which to live and Scripture defines a path to follow if we want to please God. The Christian New Testament describes a God who is loving and forgiving and who cares for people whether or not they believe in him. Here, the path to pleasing God is to simply believe in and seek a relationship with him. The Hindu faith accepts many Gods as a way to best understand all of these dimensions, and the Buddhist faith considers God to be a state of enlightenment within the individual rather than outside of him or her. To a scientist or mathematician, God might be the source of order and logic that describes how nature works. To an artist, God might be the source of inspiration about what is beautiful. To a philosopher, God might be the source of how we know right from wrong or good from evil. In some cases, it is as though God is a metaphor for the order and good in the world that we do not fully understand, but does this mean that the more we learn about the world, the less we need God? Some would say yes and would argue that humankind will eventually outgrow the need for God. To a theist, there will never be an end to God because we will never become gods ourselves.

So it is useful to consider some of the characteristics ascribed to God as a way to understand what belief in him actually means:

- God is unknowable. He is not simple or one-dimensional and we can never be perfectly sure that we know what he wants us to do.

- God is all-powerful. He does not make mistakes although we may not be able to tell why things are the way they are.

- God cares about the world, and he cares about everything in it. God created the world, but he also created us. We are in the world with the ability to make creation better or worse. He wants us to do the best we can to make it better.

- God understands in ways we cannot. He forgives our faults as long as we believe in him and seek forgiveness. Belief in God requires humility about our own limitations, but it also requires confidence in the abilities and tools he has given us.

- We can reflect God's presence in how we choose to live and in the choices we make.

None of the choices we make in life are as important as the choice of what we will use as our guide for life decisions. There is a reason why people with a faith in God have built so many of humankind's greatest accomplishments. This is not to say that people do not get things wrong a lot of the time. Faith in God does not guarantee happiness or success. For those with religious faith, it does provide help when they are unhappy and when they fail. God may have created the world, but people created religion, so religion is not and can never be perfect. The choice before us is whether to make religion better or to reject it entirely. But rejecting it means we need to accept some other moral guide for our lives. We simply cannot get through life without making moral choices. The issue is how to best do this.

Earlier we encountered the story of Dietrich Bonhoeffer, the German theologian who was executed by the Nazis at the end of World War II. At the beginning of his book *Ethics*, Bonhoeffer wrote:

> The knowledge of good and evil seems to be the aim of all ethical reflection. The first task of Christian ethics is to invalidate this knowledge. In launching this attack on the underlying assumptions of all other ethics, Christian ethics stands so completely alone that it becomes questionable whether there is any purpose of speaking of Christian ethics at all. But if one does so notwithstanding, that can only mean that Christian ethics claims to discuss the origin of the whole problem of ethics, and thus professes to be a critique of all ethics simply as ethics.[5]

Bonhoeffer went on to explain that human beings cannot fully understand good and evil or right and wrong on their own accord. To theists, these distinctions come from God and understanding right and wrong begins with understanding God. In a way, they are two ways of saying the same thing.

Relationship with God

In his book *Mere Christianity*, C.S. Lewis argued that people have an innate sense of right and wrong, that we are hard-wired with a notion of what is fair and just.[6] Lewis saw evidence of God in this innate sense. His writings suggest that he thought our consciences come from God, that most of us feel guilty when we wrong another person, and that we try to be "good people" because of God's influence in the world. To those with religious faith, there seems to be evidence of God everywhere. To those without religious faith, such beliefs seem superstitious. It is useful to consider carefully what Lewis meant by evidence of God. Examining the world around us, he found a beautiful order in nature, and more often than not,

5. Bonhoeffer, *Ethics*, 17.
6. Lewis, *Mere Christianity*, 17.

this order can be described in mathematical terms. The more we learn about the cosmos or about the natural world, the more striking this order seems to be. So Lewis found evidence of God in the natural world around us. There are also countless examples of the world being made a better place by acts of love and human kindness. No matter how bad things might be, one can always find good in the world. To theists, such goodness comes from God. To those without religious faith, goodness is either a random occurrence or the work of humankind. But humankind is also capable of remarkable cruelty. Bad things happen in the world. Injustice is common. So this leaves us with the question of whether these bad things also come from God.

Perhaps the greatest challenge to religious faith is to explain why bad things happen to good people. If God is all-powerful, then why do evil and injustice exist in the first place? Religious people might explain evil and injustice as coming from Satan, but this only raises the question of why an all-powerful God allows Satan to exist. So people are often stuck on the apparent contradiction between an all-powerful God and the presence of evil and injustice in the world. Theists might respond that evil and injustice exist because the world and those of us who live in it are imperfect, not because God is imperfect. To them, God put us here in the first place to overcome such things, and we cannot do this without his help. So it may be that simply believing that God exists is not enough. We also need to spend our lives trying to learn about him and striving to understand exactly what we should do with the short lives we are given. This is really the same thing as saying that we need to study and learn how to live "good" lives. If we are theists, it is up to us to show the presence of God in how we live and to carry out his work in making the world better. This is what it means to have a relationship with God. It means to have a relationship with goodness and to live in such a way as to lessen evil and injustice. We cannot know God, so we cannot know what true goodness is. But we can try. We can seek his help and we can join with others in this work.

If you choose not to believe in God, you can still try to live a good life. You can still work with others to fight against evil and injustice. You can still be trustworthy to your friends and forgiving to your enemies. But it seems hard to explain why you do these things. How do you know if your idea of a good life is really good? Can we really know goodness while denying that there is a source of that goodness? Maybe you have historical figures you admire and choose to model your life after. Perhaps you see virtue in the lives of Martin Luther King Jr. or Mahatma Gandhi or are inspired by the words of the American Constitution. Maybe you incorporate their examples into your own ideas of "good." But what would happen if you could actually have a conversation with King or Gandhi? Where do you suppose their ideas of right and wrong came from? Martin Luther King Jr. was a Christian minister and Gandhi was a devout Hindu. Would they tell you their ideas were their own or would they tell you their ideas arose from their religious beliefs? If you think the source of goodness exists in people, it also becomes pretty hard to explain why we get it wrong so often. Maybe the most important point is this: human beings cannot really be the original source of good. All of us started as children and learned from adults in our lives. If we see good in others, should we give all the credit to them or are we seeing God revealed through them? Theists generally define God as the origin of good. Atheists and agnostics will need another explanation.

Living with Integrity

> "He does not believe that does not live according to his belief."—Sigmund Freud[7]

Earlier we discussed the notion that those around us can only judge our beliefs by considering our actions. We might claim we believe that lying is wrong, but our belief is judged by whether or not we lie. As previously defined, this connection between what we believe and how we live is called *integrity*. We live with

7. Goodreads, Belief Quotes.

integrity when our actions consistently match our stated beliefs. So our aesthetic beliefs are reflected by what we choose to buy. Our prognostic beliefs are reflected by how we plan for the future. Our moral beliefs are reflected by how we make choices between right and wrong. The same sort of integrity is required for those with religious beliefs. If we claim to believe in a forgiving God who wants us to be forgiving people, we need to forgive others when they harm us. If we believe in the God of the Ten Commandments, we need to obey these commandments in our own lives. To live without integrity is to be a hypocrite and nothing does more harm to people trying to make decisions about their own beliefs than witnessing the hypocrisy of others. Thus, it is a major problem when children see adults they respect living without integrity. It is also a problem when adults encounter hypocrisy. Since we learn values from others around us, particularly from people we respect and those in positions of authority, our beliefs can be undermined when their behavior belies their stated beliefs. We can view hypocrisy in two ways. We might consider the hypocrite to be violating his or her own beliefs or we might question whether or not the belief was there in the first place. Remember that we defined a belief as an opinion that determines action and that cannot be proven false. If action contradicts the belief, was the belief real or not? This may not matter much in the case of aesthetic beliefs or beliefs about the future, but the stakes are higher when we consider moral beliefs and become paramount when it comes to religious belief. If someone tells us they believe in a loving and forgiving God, but does not treat others in a loving and forgiving way, we might not just have questions about them, we might also have questions about the God they claim to revere.

This is an important point about religious belief. Our behavior needs to match the sort of God we claim to believe in. Maybe this is what Dietrich Bonhoeffer meant when he wrote that Christian ethics professes to be a critique of all ethics simply as ethics. To a person of religious faith, God, not human beings, defines right and wrong. So a religious person living without integrity with their faith can undermine the faith of others. Believing in God means living in such a way as to reveal God to others. But make no mistake about it, when held to the standards of God, we are all hypocrites, and our hypocrisy causes others to wonder about our beliefs and also to wonder about our God. This then is one of the greatest threats to religious belief. When people kill in the name of religion, religion can get the blame. If you really listen to the arguments of atheists and agnostics, they are often hung up on the chasm that exists between professed religious belief and the behavior of those professing those beliefs. They blame religion for the hypocrisy of the religious rather than blaming the hypocrites themselves. The challenge of integrity can also be a barrier to professing religious faith in the first place. If you claim to be a Christian or a Muslim, you make a commitment to live in accordance with your faith and can easily find yourself having to explain acts of hypocrisy by you or by others who claim the same faith. When you really think about it, maybe it's better to avoid commitment in the first place. Thus, there are lots of atheists and agnostics in the world.

So, in the end, what are we to make of all of this? Forming beliefs and using them as a guide to making life decisions make up a major part of what it means to be a human being. Our lives are full of choices that can only be made if we have values by which to judge the options. These choices can be small, every-day decisions, or they can be momentous choices with life-altering consequences. Beliefs do not arise from nowhere. We learn them from our parents, our role models, our peers, and our communities. Doing the right thing is not a given; sometimes the best choice is far from clear. Making the world a better place requires action on our part and that action depends on what we do and do not believe. This requires careful consideration from all of us. Our beliefs will be tested and can be strong only if we work to make them strong.

> "It is necessary to the happiness of man that he be mentally faithful to himself. Infidelity does not consist in believing, or in disbelieving, it consists in professing to believe what he does not believe."—Thomas Paine, The Age of Reason[8]

8. Goodreads, Belief Quotes.

PART III

Changing Beliefs

6

How Beliefs are Changed

In discussing the nature of adult beliefs in chapter 2, we noted that beliefs can and should change over time and that this process is both necessary and healthy for adult faith. We also discussed the notion that it can be a problem if beliefs change too easily or if they fail to change as new information becomes available. So it is now time to think more carefully about how beliefs change. To do this, we will require some additional definitions. *Marketing* is defined as the action or business of promoting and selling products. In the context of belief, marketing is the active process of trying to change the aesthetic beliefs of others. *Propaganda* is information, especially of a biased or misleading nature, designed to change the political or social beliefs of another person. Propaganda has a generally negative connotation and is usually viewed as different from education in that *education* is supposed to be unbiased and focused on the transmission of knowledge. *Proselytism* is the attempt to change the religious beliefs of another person and *evangelism* is defined more narrowly as the spreading of the Christian gospel by public speaking or personal witness. Although both proselytism and evangelism relate to a process of trying to change the religious and moral beliefs of others, proselytism has a generally negative connotation while evangelism is sometimes thought of in a more positive sense. All of these terms have something in common: they all refer to a process of influencing the beliefs of others. Some people might argue that education is about knowledge and not belief, and this is a point well taken. But what is taught in an educational program and how the teaching is done can profoundly affect the beliefs of students. This is why there is so much controversy over the content of textbooks and curricula in the public schools. What one person deems education can sometimes be seen by others as propaganda. Similarly, evangelism to one observer might be considered proselytism to another. So it seems clear that there is a lot going on in our lives that relates to forming and changing beliefs.

To make better sense of this, we might separate our discussion into how this change process happens for different types of belief. We can then discuss how this relates to our own beliefs, how we can best help children and adolescents in the formation of their beliefs, and how we can influence the beliefs of other adults. It goes without saying that changing the beliefs of others can be a dangerous business, raising important questions about how and when we can be justified in doing this. But the fact is that we are constantly exposed to ideas in day-to-day life that either support or undermine our beliefs. For our beliefs to be legitimate and for them to be strong, we need to understand how this process works.

Changing Aesthetic Beliefs

One cannot turn on the television or access the Internet without encountering attempts to change what we know and what we believe. Marketing, or commercial advertising, is ubiquitous in our culture. In our discussion about how beliefs change, marketing can be considered to be a direct or indirect attempt to change our aesthetic beliefs by informing us of choices and by influencing how we think about those choices. Billions of dollars are spent each year on marketing campaigns and the business community usually considers this money to be well spent for one simple reason:

marketing works. Most of us think we can just ignore ads and commercials, but the evidence suggests otherwise. We generally underestimate the impact of these efforts on us and just accept that we are constantly being sold products and services. In spite of marketing's powerful influence, we tend to hold it to rather low ethical standards. If a car dealer tells us that the cars on his lot are the best in town, we do not really expect this to be objectively true. We understand that people selling a product will present the product in a favorable light, and we do not consider such statements to be dishonest in the same way we might if a teacher told students the same thing in a classroom. Telling the truth is somehow defined differently in a commercial context. Why is this the case? Perhaps it is different because we allow it to be different. We do not immediately walk out of a car dealership when the sales person makes such a statement. We have a social acceptance that selling is different from educating. Of course this makes it harder when marketing efforts conflate the two.

What are the techniques used in marketing campaigns that make them so effective? Consider these common examples:

- *Name recognition*: This technique involves just putting the product or service into our awareness, making us familiar with its name. Sometimes this is done with visual images like signs, and sometimes it involves auditory stimuli such as musical jingles. This technique is based on the idea that frequent repetition of a name or an idea will lead others to accept the concept. For many years, companies have paid substantial fees just to have their products appear in movies or television shows. They do this because just seeing the product increases consumer awareness about it and improves sales.

- *Value arguments*: This involves statements about cost savings and the use of sales to convince potential purchasers that they will get a good deal. This technique can be used to make the consumer feel like they will receive special treatment under certain conditions, thereby increasing their urgency about purchasing the product.

- *Desirable or undesirable association*: This technique involves associating the product or service with a famous person or popular activity. We tend to buy products that are used by someone we admire or that are associated with a desirable outcome. Thus, athletic shoes are often sold by having them associated with a winning team or a successful athlete, and physically attractive actors might be paid to sell cosmetics. Sometimes, a marketing effort will try to associate a competing product with a person or concept that has a poor reputation.

- *Crowd appeal*: A product is generally desirable if we think everyone else is using it, so marketing will sometimes seek to convince us that the product is popular, particularly with our friends and associates. The use of crowd appeal can create a sense of joining a popular trend by adopting a product or concept. Similarly, the target of marketing can be made to feel left out if they do not join those choosing the product.

- *Discrediting the competition*: Sometimes marketing seeks to discredit our other choices in order to make one product more appealing than those being discredited. This can be done by attacking a competing product or idea or by attacking a person or group of people who support it.

- *Provide evidence*: Marketing will sometimes provide evidence that a particular product or service works better than its competition. Sometimes this evidence is honest and unbiased, but sometimes it is one-sided and selective.

- *Provide testimony*: Marketing can also use testimony from trusted sources such as professionals or academics to gain the trust of the consumer. An advertisement for toothpaste might cite its endorsement by the American Dental Association for example. Testimony can also be used to attack a competing product or concept.

- *Emotional appeals*: Some marketing efforts seek to associate a product with a desirable emotional state depicting people using the product as happy or comfortable. We are more likely to buy a product that makes us feel safe or loved or content. Emotional appeals can also play on fear, anxiety, or bigotry. For example, home security systems can be marketed by playing on our fear of crime.

Although the use of marketing to change the aesthetic beliefs of consumers might seem to be a simple example when compared to political propaganda, there is irrefutable evidence that it is effective in manipulating and influencing our beliefs about what tastes good, looks good, sounds good, or feels good. Recognizing marketing in the world around us is a good way to learn how to be careful about how we allow ourselves to be influenced. In some cases, marketing efforts can also be used to subtly influence other beliefs while they are overtly selling a product or service. If we can understand this process better, we can build stronger aesthetic beliefs and prevent ourselves from being influenced by deceptive arguments.

Changing Political Beliefs

If we improve our understanding of marketing, it should also help us to recognize attempts to change our political beliefs, because many of the same techniques are used. In some ways, the stakes seem higher for political beliefs. Political beliefs influence how our society and government work, not just how we spend our money. At a national level, our political choices can affect world peace. At a local level, political beliefs can influence our schools, our communities, and social support programs for our neighbors and for us.

The term *propaganda* is often used to describe attempts to change the political beliefs of others, but it actually originates from a religious context. In 1622, Pope Gregory XV created a committee of cardinals called the Congregation for the Propagation of Faith (in Latin the *Congregatio de Propaganda Fide*). At that time in history, it was generally accepted that Christians should work to bring others into a faith in Christ. So it probably seemed quite natural that the church's efforts be organized behind this goal. But there was no a priori agreement about how this should be done. At its simplest level, spreading the Christian faith might just involve education. But simple education can easily devolve into more coercive methods of persuasion. For example, missionaries might tell poorly educated people that they will be damned to an eternity of suffering if they do not accept specific religious beliefs, and this might even be based on an honest belief on the part of the missionaries that this is true. So history is filled with attempts to proselytize using fear as a method of persuasion. It is not hard to see how this might be coercive and mean-spirited. Thus the term *propaganda* came to be viewed as the use of deception to change the beliefs of others. Later, techniques of propaganda have been used to spread political and social beliefs, and it is in this context that the word is most often used today.

Techniques of propaganda might include attempts to play on the fear and bigotry of others by convincing people that those not like them should not be trusted. Propagandists might spread false rumors and conspiracy theories or incite racial hatred to accomplish political goals. These techniques are common in the world around us and they are not limited to dictatorships in third-world countries. If you listen carefully, you can find these techniques being used in modern political debates and election campaigns. How can we be protected from propaganda's influence? First, we can learn to identify it when we see and hear it. Learning about how propaganda has been used in history can help us to recognize it. Second, we can learn to ask questions and to engage in honest debate. We can learn to distrust arguments that appeal to bigotry or vilify opposing points of view. Third, we can recognize that we are all susceptible to such techniques just as we are susceptible to marketing when it comes to our purchasing decisions. But the best protection against propaganda is to have a strong system of moral beliefs—to know right from wrong—when engaging in political discourse. A strong sense of our own beliefs makes it easier to consider openly the ideas of others while still retaining our own.

Carefully listening to the ideas of others can also help us to adapt and change our beliefs as new information or different perspectives become available. Strong moral beliefs and an educated mind are our best protections against propaganda.

Changing Social Beliefs

"We can believe what we choose. We are answerable for what we choose to believe."—John Henry Newman[1]

Earlier, we discussed how social beliefs were manipulated to instill Nazi ideology in Germany in the 1930s. History is filled with examples of how morally reprehensible ideas can be tolerated within social groups. The forced relocation of Native American tribes from the eastern United States in the 1830s and the widespread acceptance of slavery in America for over a hundred years are other examples of this phenomenon. These historical events took place in spite of the fact that most Americans at the time considered themselves to be Christians. (Atheists might argue that religious faith made it easier to depersonalize those not sharing the same faith.) While many opposed these decisions, the opposition was ineffective at stopping what are now widely recognized as atrocious violations of human rights. These examples make it clear that others can manipulate our political and social beliefs, but that does not make it easy to understand how and why this is possible. Appeals to greed and to fear are common themes in these stories. Changing the social beliefs of others often requires the use of sophisticated communication techniques. It is probably easier when the community being influenced is poorly educated or experiencing hard times. Perhaps it is harder to care for others when we are ourselves unemployed, or hungry, or feeling unsafe.

Social beliefs can also change in positive ways. Americans believe in democracy and in the principles outlined in the Declaration of Independence. If we do not believe in these things, then others might question whether we are really American. Since

1. Goodreads, Belief Quotes.

belonging to a cultural group or community is important to human beings, the social beliefs of our communities are a powerful force in determining what we believe as individuals. While we might not have always lived up to these values, having them written down can help us to see the inconsistency. Yet for over a hundred years, many people in America had strong social beliefs about racial differences. These beliefs were reinforced by laws that prohibited African Americans from going to the same schools or eating in the same restaurants as white Americans. The way we talk about race and the social order of our culture perpetuates racism as a social belief. There were sometimes real consequences for those opposing these beliefs. Protesters in the civil rights movement of the 1960s were confronted with arrest, violence, and social isolation when they took a stand against segregation and racial discrimination. Eventually, it became unacceptable to openly practice racism, but this did not cause racist beliefs to disappear, and they continue to be expressed in more private and subtle ways. Overt racism still resurfaces from time to time in very public ways. Nevertheless, something about the civil rights movement caused American social values to change. Overt racism went from being accepted by the majority to being rejected by the majority and this process continues to evolve today.

So it is important to understand how change in social beliefs comes about. In general, the process begins when a minority of people choose to challenge an established social system. This minority persists over time in spite of opposition and eventually begins to win over converts to the cause by creating arguments that appeal to the larger social group. Sometimes these arguments are about moral values, but sometimes they appeal to greed, intolerance, or fear. The social belief begins to change when arguments of the minority begin to convert the majority. Sometimes this works and sometimes it does not. In the case of Martin Luther and the Protestant Reformation of the sixteenth-century, the reform movement worked. In the case of the American colonists declaring independence from the British crown, the reform movement worked. But in the case of the German opposition to the Nazi party, the reform did not work until the Nazis were defeated in the Second World War. It took over a century and the Civil War for opposition to slavery to prevail. History is filled with examples of successful and unsuccessful social reform movements. Being right does not guarantee success. Being popular does not guarantee success. Faith in God does not guarantee success. But consider for a moment what we mean by success. Maybe success is not always what we expect it to be. Few of us today are not inspired by the courage and moral rectitude of Dietrich Bonhoeffer even though the Nazis executed him as a traitor. Did Bonhoeffer consider his efforts to be successful in the last moments of his life? His letters from prison suggest that he did. For him, the rightness of his cause was not decided by the short-term outcome of his actions. Changing social beliefs is a serious and sometimes dangerous business. Perhaps the leaders of the American civil rights movement were able to learn from Bonhoeffer's principled persistence. Maybe this was the real purpose of his entire life. Maybe there is no way he could have fully understood this during his life. Maybe that is the point.

7

Changing Moral and Religious Beliefs

I n our earlier discussion about religious beliefs, we noted the risk of moral absolutism in religious belief systems. If a Christian believes that God can be understood only through a belief in Jesus Christ as his Son, then it can be easy for him or her to discount beliefs in God that do not follow this path. Just as no one can prove that our religious belief is wrong, neither can we prove that other religions are wrong. Among the most common arguments in support of atheism is the seeming intolerance of mainstream religions. At its worst, proselytism can undermine the very notion of a loving God, but this does not mean that we cannot talk with one another about religion or moral values. In fact, moral and religious beliefs can be strong only if we talk with one another about them, and this does not mean talking only with people who agree with us.

Changing our Own Moral Beliefs

One characteristic of a strong moral belief is that it survives the test of time. Our beliefs are our guide to making choices in our lives, and we are faced with moral choices every day. How much value we place on honesty directly influences whether or not we tell the truth when confronting an opportunity to lie. We cannot claim to believe in democracy unless we are willing to value everyone's voice in the democratic process. And yet elections are often won by whoever inspires their own supporters to vote in greater numbers than the supporters of their opponents. If we believe in practicing charity for those less fortunate than we are, it has ramifications for our daily choices about how to treat the poor or the sick. So our beliefs about right and wrong are challenged every single day by choices that confront us. Strong beliefs become stronger when they are tested. Weak beliefs are undermined when we fail to live up to them. But how can we tell when one of our moral beliefs is false? Perhaps we claim to have a belief that lying is wrong, but we still frequently lie. Does that mean the belief is false or does it just mean that we just fail to live up to it?

This takes us back to our earlier discussion about the relationship between belief and behavior. It might help at this point to clarify a couple of points. First, we have defined a belief as a proposition we assume to be true when choosing how to behave. If we do not behave in accordance with a belief, it is not a belief we truly hold. This does not make it a morally bad belief, it just means that it fails to satisfy our definition of what a belief is. So a person who lies frequently cannot be said to truly believe in telling the truth. Second, integrity does not always need to be absolute for our belief to be genuine. Is our belief in honesty immediately proven false the first time we tell a lie? Not necessarily. Maybe it matters what we learn from this inconsistency. None of us is perfect. All of us fail the test of integrity from time to time. The key concept here is that we learn from the experience and either strengthen or abandon a belief that we fail to follow with the choices we make.

So now we can consider two ways by which our own beliefs are adapted over time. The first is when we learn from having the belief tested. Consistently failing to make choices as guided by a belief should call the legitimacy of the belief into question. But this requires reflection on our part. Perhaps we believe in always telling the truth, but we experience undesired outcomes when we follow this belief in all circumstances and this, in turn, causes us to modify the belief to account for different conditions. In effect, we learn from experience how and when to modify the belief conditionally. Our experiences can also strengthen a belief whether or not the consequences are desirable for us and those we care about. A second way for us to modify our beliefs is by learning from others. All of us tend to emulate those we respect, and we also try to avoid emulating those we do not respect. So, the beliefs and resulting behavior of other people can serve as lessons for us. Such lessons can be based on what we see others doing in their own lives, and they can also be based on lessons from history and literature. In any case, our beliefs evolve only when we are capable of moral reflection about our own actions and the actions of others.

A core characteristic of adult belief systems is the ability to adapt over time. Human beings are constantly learning. We learn new facts. We learn from experience. And we are all capable of moral learning.

Influencing the Moral and Religious Beliefs of Others

> "We are always trying to convert people to a belief in our own explanation of the universe. We think that the more people there are who believe as we do, the more certain it will be that what we believe is the truth. But it doesn't work that way at all."—Paulo Coelho, The Pilgrimage[1]

Is it ever morally correct to try to change the moral or religious beliefs of other people? Is there a difference between passively influencing the beliefs of others and actively seeking ways to change those beliefs? Perhaps the best way to influence the beliefs of others is to live with integrity with our own beliefs. The simple fact is that we cannot change the beliefs of other people; only they can

---

1. Goodreads, Belief Quotes.

do this. But we certainly can influence the beliefs of others. The most powerful ways to teach our children to tell the truth is never to lie to them and to allow consequences to happen when they tell lies. The same is true of adults. People learn more from what we do than from what we say. So the first principle to follow when considering the beliefs of other people is to care about them and to live your own life with integrity. Setting a positive example does not require us to judge anyone but ourselves.

This does not mean that we should not be willing to talk about beliefs with other people in our lives. Sharing our own beliefs and the reasons why we hold them does not have to be judgmental. Valuing our own beliefs does not require us to discount the beliefs of others. In fact, we might even have an obligation to help other people find a set of moral and religious values in their own lives. But what should we do when someone has an unconditionally bad belief? Morally wrong social beliefs can be stopped only if we confront them. So openly racist behavior must not be tolerated just to avoid appearing intolerant. The problem here is that it can be hard to know which social beliefs are unconditionally bad. Surely this is not just a matter of social acceptance. Slavery was always wrong even though it took a long time for people to agree about this unconditionally. This means that we sometimes must be judgmental about beliefs even as we try to avoid being judgmental about people.

So consider some of the following as ways to avoid imposing your moral beliefs on others:

- When sharing your religious and moral beliefs with others, make first-person statements about what you believe and why you believe it.

- When talking with others about religious and moral beliefs, be curious about what they believe and why. Listen carefully and reflect what you understand them to be saying.

- Ask questions about the beliefs of others while avoiding value judgments about them. Judging people is God's job, not ours, but you can and must oppose morally reprehensible beliefs. If you never oppose such beliefs, you are condoning them.

- Live in accordance with your religious and moral beliefs. Nothing undermines an argument more quickly than hypocrisy.

- Remember that you can care for a person without always agreeing with them. In fact, this distinction is centrally important in most religious traditions even though it is a commonly violated principle.

Moral and religious beliefs cannot be strong if they are held in secret and never shared. Maybe it is not necessary to openly talk about our beliefs, but it is necessary to live as examples to others. Having strong religious beliefs does not have to lead to intolerance. There are many possible paths to finding your way to moral truth or to God and we can learn a lot about God and about our own moral beliefs when we learn about the paths of others. At its best, evangelism is more about our own faith than it is about changing the faith of others. To theists, there is no boundary between religious and moral belief. Moral belief is about right and wrong, and religious belief is about God. For the theist, God is the path to understanding right and wrong. But belief in God requires humility and seeking a relationship with God requires a willingness to respect other points of view. This is certainly evident in the teachings of Jesus. It is also true in most other religious traditions. The Christian seeks to live as Jesus lived and Jesus lived with compassion and love for everyone.

PART IV

Choosing Faith

8

Prioritizing Beliefs

Thus far, we have focused on individual beliefs. We have examined how beliefs are formed and how they change, and we have created a list of categories describing various types of belief. It is now time to consider how beliefs relate to one another. All of us have many beliefs. We might believe that Diet Coke is the best soft drink (an aesthetic belief) and we might believe that representative democracy is the best form of government (a political or social belief). Clearly, these two beliefs are not of equal importance. So now we need to consider how beliefs relate to one another and how they are prioritized. The most important of our beliefs are those that have the greatest impact on how we choose to live our lives, so it matters how we prioritize them. The collection of beliefs that are most important to us can be referred to as our faith.

The Oxford dictionary defines *worship* as the feeling or expression of reverence and adoration for a deity.[1] The definition states that this word can allude to religious rites or ceremonies or to "great admiration or devotion shown towards a person or principle." If we ignore the religious connotation of this word, we

1. *New Oxford American Dictionary*, 1993.

can focus on the latter meaning. In this sense, people "worship" those beliefs that they hold in highest regard. This then raises the following question: what do you worship in your life? If you carefully think about this, your answer might include one or more of the following:

- *Wealth*: Many people measure the success of their life partly or solely on the basis of financial accomplishment. If accumulating money is how you judge success, one might say that you "worship" financial success.

- *Power*: Some people highly value power or the ability to exert control over other people. Political power, social power, and positional power over others are examples.

- *Possessions*: Similar to wealth, some people place high value on accumulating objects such as a house or a car or a collection of art.

- *Mastery*: People can worship the accumulation of skill and live their lives to become more and more accomplished in athletics or music or a particular profession.

- *Popularity*: Some people place highest value on being well liked or respected by other people. The more people like you, the more successful you are.

- *Fame*: Similar to popularity, people can highly value being known or becoming a celebrity. If more people who know who you are, then you are more successful.

- *Knowledge*: Many scholars place high value on knowing about a particular subject or field of study.

- *Family*: People can certainly prioritize their families and judge the success of their lives by the success of their parents, siblings, spouses/partners, children, or grandchildren.

- *Freedom*: Some people might place high value on being able to do whatever they want without external constraint.

- *Pleasure*: People can also place high value on personal pleasure or happiness.

- *Physical attractiveness*: Some people most highly value the attractiveness of their personal appearance to others.

- *Moral truth or goodness*: Some people place highest value on being a morally good and just person, of doing the right thing or making the right choices. Of course this necessarily requires them to choose definitions of moral correctness, justice, and goodness.

- *Religious Faith*: Finally, many people place highest value on their religious faith and seek to better understand how this should guide their lives. Again, this requires them to delve deeply into what sort of God they believe in and how they come to understand the teachings of that God.

This list is not meant to imply that we all choose just one of these options. Most people would certainly value several of the priorities on this list, and some might find their most cherished values missing from the list entirely. But the beliefs that we give highest priority in our lives, the ones we "worship," become our primary purpose or faith. They form our measures of success and the determinants of our self-worth. Another way to say this is that the beliefs we value the most become the "gods" we choose to worship. This is true of atheists, agnostics, and theists alike because the term *god* is being used here to mean the beliefs we give highest priority rather than God as a supernatural and divine entity.

Choosing a Purpose

So how do we decide about our faith? For many people, this does not seem like a choice. We are the product of our upbringing and our experiences, both positive and negative. Sometimes circumstances and environment seem to predetermine our purpose, and we feel we have no control or choice in what will happen next. So one way of choosing a faith is not to choose at all and to live life on a day-to-day basis without a clear purpose. Maybe we have never seen anyone living in any other way. Maybe we do not think our choices can possibly matter. But consider for a moment the ramifications of such an approach. Is this not the same thing as saying our life has no purpose? Not making a choice about our faith is in fact choosing not to choose. A life lived without considering its purpose seems unlikely to produce success by any measure in the end. One of the defining characteristics of human beings is that we alone among all of the creatures on earth are capable of considering purpose. We can all choose because we are human beings. So the first step is to take responsibility for the choice.

The moment we begin to contemplate the choice of our life purpose is the moment we confront the vast complexity of the choice. We are surrounded by other people each chasing after their own notion of purpose, and we are greatly influenced by the social mores of those closest to us, particularly our families and communities. We have already discussed how the beliefs of children begin to take shape under the influence of parents and other adult role models. These same influences directly affect how we prioritize our beliefs, and it is from these priorities that our faith arises. We have also emphasized that the beliefs of children are challenged in adolescence and must be confirmed or revised in adulthood. The same is true when it comes to the relative priority we place on each belief. When we come face to face with this choice, we encounter family, community, and social expectations. In most communities, we are "supposed to" value moral correctness more highly than wealth or power. We are "supposed to" value knowledge more than popularity or fame. In fact, we encounter gaping breaches in integrity all around us as "successful" people tell us they most highly value one set of beliefs while living their lives in direct pursuit of others. Nearly everyone would rather be rich than poor, but not everyone places wealth at the top of his or her list of life goals. So we tend to emulate those we admire, and we try to be different from those we do not respect even while we struggle to determine exactly where our admiration and respect come from in the first place. The process of choosing a faith for your life is hard work and requires conscious thought. It can be guided by studying the choices of others and by talking with family and friends. But it matters what we study and whom we consult. As with all of our beliefs, we need to continually reassess and modify our faith as things change around us, but we also have to take responsibility for and maintain integrity with our choices.

Earlier we discussed the differences between internal and external loci of control. For those with an external locus of control, life priorities can seem to result entirely from circumstance. To them, faith can seem like an outcome more than a choice. So many people live their lives without spending much time thinking about faith, and they might even think that choosing a purpose is a waste of time. This can work out fine for a while. We can accumulate wealth or be elected to political office without really making such things conscious goals. We can do well in school, advance in our careers, and earn the respect of our peers without considering why we care about these things. But sooner or later, we have to decide how we feel about the lives we are living, and we need criteria by which to judge our own successes and failures. The benchmarks by which we make these assessments are necessarily derived from our most cherished beliefs and goals. Accomplishments can seem pretty shallow when we cannot answer the question of why they matter to us. So even those with an extreme external locus of control will sooner or later have to consider their choice of faith.

Those with an internal locus of control tend to view life on the basis of the choices they make and the skills they use to react to circumstances. For them, purpose might be considered earlier in life, but that does not mean they always do so with depth of thought. Our choices are always influenced by circumstances beyond our control, so maybe our purpose changes when we encounter some opportunities and not others. Regardless of our locus of control, it can be hard to arrive at a central purpose for life without continuously reassessing core beliefs. So finding faith is a work in progress from the start of our lives until the end. None of us know when our life will end. Most of us do not often think about how we will know whether or not our lives have been successful. But virtually no one can state honestly that he or she does not care about this question. So choosing a purpose and living life with fidelity to that choice are hard to avoid when we think about how our lives will be viewed by us in our last days and by others when we are gone.

For most of our lives, it can seem costly indeed to explicitly choose a purpose. First, there is the problem of having to face failure if you are not successful based on the purpose we've chosen. Second, we are likely to encounter criticism regardless of our choice. If our chosen purpose is financial wealth, friends and family might be disappointed that we did not choose family or religious faith. If we choose family or religious faith, we might not end up with as many possessions as our neighbors. There is also the issue of regretting the choices we decided not to make. Once our children are grown, we cannot get back the time we lost while focusing on our jobs or our professional reputations. So it can seem risky to choose, even for the most ardent believer in internal locus of control. We make choices about how to use our time, our money, and our skills every single day. Having a clearly chosen purpose can guide these choices, but it can also cause us to feel guilty when we make these daily choices without integrity to that purpose. Thus, there are real consequences from either choosing or not choosing a faith for our lives.

9

Moral Purpose

No matter what we choose as the central purpose of our lives, we still have to come to terms with moral beliefs. We still need criteria by which to evaluate our day-to-day choices and our moral beliefs will work best if they fit with our faith. So let's consider a couple of examples to make this clearer.

Alice is a person who most highly values wealth and financial success. She chooses a college based on where she could get a good education for a career in business and soon starts her own business where she prioritizes her income potential. Alice is most likely to make moral choices based on the consequences of those choices for her financial well-being. The right choice is the one that best supports her business. The wrong choice is the one that hurts her business. In the short term, this might make her prone to cutting corners to maximize profits. But this could hurt her business in the long term by damaging the market reputation of the products she produces. Alice might care deeply about the plight of the poor, but she has to balance her charity with the negative impact this might have on her bank account balance.

Henry is a person who prioritizes his family over everything else. Henry chooses a career based on having time to spend with his spouse and children. He sees his work as a means to an end and not the main purpose of his life, and he makes choices about work with the needs of his family as his paramount goal. Henry might miss opportunities to advance at work because of his focus on family, but this is balanced by his family's needs for financial support. Henry might also care deeply about the poor, but he will make choices about charity based on the needs of his family and the values he wants his children to learn.

Joan is a person whose primary purpose in life is her religious faith. She was raised as a Christian and attends church regularly while seeking to understand God's purpose for her life. She has a career and a family, so she also has financial concerns and family priorities. Joan makes the choices in her life based on what she believes to be God's priorities. She evaluates job choices based on the teachings of her faith, and she tries to raise her children to value their own religious faith. Joan also cares deeply about the poor, but she will make choices about charity based on the teachings of Jesus Christ. Jesus lived a life without material wealth and his teachings suggest that care for those less fortunate should be a primary goal for Christians. This sometimes creates challenges with regards to Joan's own financial well-being, but she believes that helping others is central to her life purpose. So she might make greater sacrifices in helping them than would seem prudent to Alice or Henry. Joan does not think this makes her better than Alice or Henry because Jesus also taught humility and compassion for others.

These three stories are admittedly simplistic, but they underscore the importance of how people think about the central purposes of their lives. When their choices are initially examined, there is nothing inherently wrong with any of them. When considered over the course of their entire lives, a different picture might emerge. What will Alice have at the end of her life? If she is successful, she will have money and property, and she might have built a successful business to leave her children. Her children might have learned the importance of hard work from her, but they might also have learned that they were not her most important priorities. Alice is likely to be financially comfortable, but she cannot take any of these assets with her when she dies. Will Alice be satisfied with this on her deathbed? What about Henry? If Henry is successful, his children will get a good education and enter adulthood feeling loved and supported. They will have learned from him about the importance of family, and they might be more likely to place a high priority on their own families in adulthood. The children might see and appreciate his self-sacrifice, but they might also learn from him that people outside of the family are less important. Henry might not have given his children as much property as Alice could give hers, but he has made them feel loved. But has he really taught them to love others? Does this matter to him? Finally, what about Joan? Joan will have spent her life trying to demonstrate her faith to her children and to her community. If she is successful, she will have impacted the lives of others through her generosity and compassion. She might have regrets about her finances, but she will have been an example of Christian love to everyone she has met. She might wonder at the end of her life if she has fully lived up to God's purpose for her, but she would have spent her life trying. What will Joan's children have learned from her? Joan will have taught her children that there are more important things in life than money or family or self-interest. She will have shown them how God might work through their own lives just as he worked through hers. Just like the children of Alice and Henry, Joan's children may not have learned these lessons. But maybe they have.

What are the real differences between Alice, Henry, and Joan? Perhaps all have been successful, but only Joan has chosen a set of moral values to be her purpose. Alice has chosen personal rewards as her goal. She has prioritized herself. Henry has placed his priority on his children, but our children are, in a sense, extensions of ourselves. In placing their needs ahead of others, he has taught his children to do the same. We live in a culture that places high value on family, but we rarely think about the inherent problems that can arise if this is our primary purpose. Only Joan has truly placed the needs of others at the center of her life. Is this solely because she is a Christian? Perhaps not. Christians do not have a monopoly on altruism. Nevertheless, Joan has tried to define and pursue a moral purpose in making life choices and tried to live as an example of selflessness. In her case, this moral purpose came from her religious faith. She did not base her life choices on her own moral code; she based them on what she believed to be the will of God.

Perhaps we might evaluate the lives of these three people using Kant's categorical imperative. Recall that the first part of his imperative was always to make a moral choice that we would like everyone in the world to make in the same situation. Would we want everyone in the world to live as Alice has lived? If we do, then the world is a marketplace and we are all in it for ourselves. Similarly, do we want everyone to live as Henry has lived? If we do, then the world is divided into tribal groups with people caring mostly about people who are related to them. If everyone in the world lived like Joan, the world would be a more caring and selfless place. Which sort of world is best? How much do we care about the sort of world we spend our lives trying to create?

Is it Really our Choice that Matters?

The world really does not work very well when we think it is all about our choices and our beliefs. No matter how much we struggle to find our purpose, we are still left with the question of whether our choices really matter in the end. Our lives are short. With billions of people on the earth, what can any individual life really accomplish? That is the problem with personal choice being the basis of our philosophy. Is life really about what we choose or is there more to it? If life is not about us, is it simply a matter of altruistically caring for others? Few would argue that the world would be better if everyone was in it only for himself or herself. The problem here is that while we might collectively be better off in an altruistic world, none of us have much incentive to be altruistic as individuals. The only altruist in an entirely selfish world would probably not fare well. Or would they? So finally we arrive at the central issue when it comes to faith. The inherent contradiction between the sort of world we wish for and the sort of world we live in brings us once again to religion.

We spend our lives learning about, adopting, and modifying beliefs, beliefs about simple things like our taste in food and about more complex things like our concepts of right and wrong. If we take this one step further, we prioritize our beliefs and we choose those most important to us as our faith. Perhaps we even choose a moral code as our central purpose. But when this is considered over the long term, we struggle to see how our lives can be successful. Maybe we need to think more deeply about what success means. Is it possible that no philosophy of life based on our own sense of purpose can lead to a better world? If life is not about us, but a central moral purpose to our lives still matters, then life must be about something else entirely. So now we come to the heart of the matter.

IO

Choosing Religious Faith

It is beyond the scope of this book to review all of the world's religions. There are plenty of other books that do this. Our purpose here is to explain why it is impossible to resolve the contradictions of our world if our tools include only our own wits and the ideas of other human beings. For many, it seems hard to believe in an all-knowing and all-powerful God and it seems entirely unclear how such a belief might make life any better or any easier. So the best thing for me to do is to fall back on what I know and believe about my own life. In the preface of this book, I shared that I am a Christian and was raised in the Lutheran Church. Like everyone else, I am biased by my own experiences. But I am also informed by those experiences. In fact, I have little to share beyond those things that I know and that I believe. My religious faith is important to me, but it is not an unquestioning acceptance of what my parents taught me or what I heard in church growing up. Instead, it is the product of daily study and careful thought. It is based on what I have experienced in my life as a husband, father, and physician. It is based on my observations of how other people make choices. I have delivered hundreds of babies in my work as a family physician. I have also cared for hundreds of dying people. Questions of faith are more obvious at the start and the end of life, and I have been fortunate to share in the lives of my patients. I learn from their successes, but I also learn from their fears and disappointments. This is personal for me, so the story needs to be told personally.

The first question is why do I believe in God, but this immediately leads to the question of what I mean when I refer to God. Here we are talking about God as a supernatural and all-powerful entity not simply as a set of beliefs I choose to worship. There are three critical dimensions to my definition of God. They are:

1. God is the organizing force behind everything in the universe. He is the explanation behind the laws of physics and of nature. This is the facet of God that has been so important to scientists like Einstein. In this sense, God created the universe, but, to me, creation is not a completed act. Everything I know about science leads me to believe that creation is ongoing. The universe is expanding, and biological species are evolving. I believe the actions of human beings can have a measurable impact on nature, so we are actors in God's ongoing creation. We should try to help to build a more perfect physical world to the extent we can and to the extent we can know what this is. The God of creation is a God of laws and rules. This includes the laws of nature, and it includes laws given to guide human decision making. So I try to follow the Ten Commandments to the extent that I can understand their full meaning. My reaction to the God of creation is *awe*. I see God's work when I look at the stars at night and when I consider the dignity and resilience of the people I meet in my life.

2. God is the source of goodness and morality. To me, God defines what is right and wrong. I try to understand this, but to know right and wrong perfectly is to know God and God cannot be known completely. God has given us the life of his son as a moral example for our lives and to show his love

93

for us. Captured in the New Testament, Jesus' moral teaching centers on just two ideas, that we should love God and that we should love one another as God loves us. This means that altruism or caring for others is not my choice; it is God's choice for me and for all of us. God as the source of moral goodness also teaches us that our failures in life are forgiven as long as we maintain faith and seek forgiveness. As a believer in God as a source of moral truth, I believe that it is not my job to judge others. It is my job to care for others unconditionally, because this is what it means to love them. The New Testament Gospels are full of stories about Jesus caring for even the most undeserving people. We do not love others because they deserve it. We love them because God wants us to. My response to the God of moral goodness is *humility* because I can never live up to the standards set by Jesus. The only reason I can do anything good is because of God's grace as the source of that goodness. It is certainly true that Christians, including me, fail miserably to live up to God's standards of goodness. In fact, I see Christians behaving in direct opposition to the teachings of Jesus every day. But to me, our hypocrisy is our failing not God's. I can positively influence other people, but their choices are their own, and their accountability is to God and not to me. My response to the moral failings of others and to my own moral weakness must always be forgiveness, because that is what Jesus teaches us to do.

3. God cares about what I do with my life. If I live life well, my purpose is to make his creation more perfect, to bring his teachings to life for others, to love others unconditionally, and to seek a better understanding of him through a relationship with him. My response to this aspect of God is to feel *thankful and blessed*. This is the aspect of God that can be hardest for some people. If God is all-powerful, why should he care about me? The answer is because that is part of who God is. If God does not want a relationship with me, then he does not care about what I do or do not do. For me, God's

caring about what I do is central to my own purpose. If you believe only in the all-powerful God of creation and in the God of moral purity, you still cannot persuasively answer the question of why your own life matters. I believe my life matters, so I must believe that my God cares about my choices.

For Christians, these three aspects of God probably look pretty familiar because Christian theology considers God to be a Trinity of Father (creator), Son (moral authority), and Holy Spirit (the God who is in relationship with us). Sometimes I am bothered by how complicated the theologians can make things, but then I remember that it is a complicated business to try to understand God and theologians have spent far more time thinking about this than I have. I am interested in what they have to say about these questions. I learn from them. But I also think they sometimes make things more complicated than they need to be.

Everything about my life is connected to my religious faith. I see divine beauty when I learn about nature, and I feel close to God when I look into the night sky. The more I learn about nature, the more I learn about God. I see miracles every day in my work as a physician and am bothered by physicians who think of themselves as healers. Physicians prescribe treatment; God heals. I see the moral dimensions of every choice I make, in how I spend my time and money, and in how I treat other people. Many times an act of kindness goes unnoticed or unappreciated. But sometimes an act of kindness shows the love of God to other people. People can change their lives based on such acts. I have seen this happen in my own life. So what we do matters far more than we think. My belief in God gives my life purpose. It helps me to make hard choices. And it reveals beauty and truth to me on a daily basis.

Religious Faith as a Journey

So now I have put my own cards on the table. I cannot prove to you that God exists, but I certainly believe that the world is more beautiful to me and my life is more meaningful because I believe in him. This is no longer a logical argument; it is now a personal testimony. God has given each of us the ability to choose what to believe from the simplest aesthetic beliefs to the most profound moral choices. This freedom is among his greatest gifts to us. God wants us to choose him. He wants us to use our lives to make the world better. Perhaps he created an imperfect world just for us to work on! To be sure, much harm has been done in the name of religion. But this harm arises from the failure of people, not from the failure of God. No one who professes a belief in God can fully understand what this means because we cannot fully understand him. And if I cannot completely understand it myself, I can hardly be expected to fully explain it to you. Some people claim religious faith, but their life choices belie their words. Others profess religious faith, but fall short in the attempt to show their faith through their actions in spite of good intentions. But it is not my job to judge others. It is my job to act every day in a way that reflects my understanding of God's will. I cannot know God completely, so I cannot perfectly know his will. But I can spend my life trying to learn about God and I can try to live as an example of why my faith matters. This is why it is a mistake to think of religious faith as something you can fully attain in the short life you are given. Faith is not a destination, it is a journey that does not end before the end of your life. None of us have all the answers because none of us can have all the answers. But we can share what we have learned with each other and do the best we can.

So how might I respond to the atheist who has questions about my faith? I usually respond by asking them what they believe in and why they believe it. In my experience, atheists often have carefully thought about their beliefs and many of them can clearly articulate a faith that does not include God. But none of them can really answer the question of why they have chosen the faith they have chosen. Instead, they recite all of the failings of religion and offer examples of the hypocrisy of religious people. Their argument boils down to why they disagree with what I believe and not why their beliefs are better. Sometimes I can find religious principles in the faith of atheists. Many of them practice charity. Many care for others. Many value honesty and find religious texts to be useful guides for life. But few can convincingly defend where these ideas come from and why they think human beings can achieve moral rectitude on our own. In my own experience, most atheists have spent more time thinking about the problems of religion than about the foundations of their own beliefs. So these discussions are usually interesting, but not convincing.

How to respond to the agnostic is an altogether different challenge. The agnostic admits to not knowing about God. They tend to remain uncommitted one way or the other on questions of religion. Unlike the atheist, they have not always given much thought to faith. My first step in discussing faith with an agnostic is to share what I believe and why. The second step is to listen to their questions and doubts. The atheist has made a choice. Perhaps they will someday change their mind. But the agnostic has not made a choice. In some ways this makes them less ready to have the conversation. So patience is required.

How do I respond to a person with a religious faith that is different from my own? I always see these discussions as opportunities to learn more about God. To think that I understand God better than anyone else is completely inconsistent with the humility taught by Jesus. I have learned a lot from people of other faiths. I try not to argue with them and I try to respect their faith traditions. In many cases, I find their descriptions of God completely compatible with my own even though they use different words than I do. Christian faith does not prescribe intolerance even though intolerance seems to arise often in the behavior of Christians. So some of my most difficult discussions are with people who describe themselves as Christians.

In the end, I think it is beyond my power to change the moral and religious beliefs of other people. Only they can do this. But it is in my power to create teachable moments and to live as an example of my faith. Few find God on the first try. We are all a work in progress. Just as I have tried to master my skills as a physician, to be a good father and husband, and to live out the teachings of my faith, others are trying to figure out things too. You made a decision to read this book. Why did you do this? What were you looking for? I suspect that you are a lot like me. You are searching for meaning in your life, and you somehow know that your beliefs lie at the heart of this meaning. We are put on this earth to make God's creation a more perfect world and we spend our entire lives trying to figure out what perfect means and how best to bring about the changes the world most needs. Everything we do matters from the largest to the smallest of life decisions. That is why our lives matter and, in turn, why our beliefs matter. We live in a time where depression, drug abuse, family violence, and intolerance are widespread. The solution to all of these problems lies in acts of kindness and compassion undertaken regularly by as many people as possible. If you can agree with this, you are on the right track. Faith is a lifelong journey. You have control over your own journey, and you can start now no matter what you have done in the past.

Bibliography and Suggested Readings

Adams, Christine, and Ernest Frugé. *Why Children Misbehave and What to Do About It*. Oakland, CA: New Harbinger, 1996.

Bennett, William J. *The Book of Virtues: A Treasury of Great Moral Stories*. New York: Simon and Schuster, 1993.

Bonhoeffer, Dietrich. *The Cost of Discipleship*. New York: Collier, 1963.

———. *Ethics*. New York: Collier, 1955.

———. *Letters and Papers From Prison*. New York: Touchstone, 1997.

Christie-Seely, Janet. *Working with the Family in Primary Care: A Systems Approach to Health and Illness*. New York: Praeger, 1984.

Clifford, William K. The Ethics of Belief. http://www.uta.edu/philosophy/faculty/burgess-jackson/Clifford.pdf.

Coles, Robert. *Children of Crisis: Selections from the Five-Volume Children of Crisis Series*. New York: Little Brown, 2003.

Collins, Francis S. *The Language of God: A Scientist Presents Evidence For Belief*. New York: Simon and Schuster, 2006.

Danielson, Dennis Richard, ed. *The Book of the Cosmos: Imagining the Universe from Heraclitus to Hawking*. Cambridge, MA: Perseus, 2000.

Deci, Edward L., and Richard Flaste. *Why We Do What We Do: The Dynamics of Personal Autonomy*. New York: Grosset, 1995

Dillenberger, John, ed. *Martin Luther: Selections From His Writings*. New York: Anchor, 1962.

Durant, Will. *The Story of Philosophy*. New York: Washington Square, 1961.

Einstein, Albert. *Essays in Humanism*. New York: Philosophical Library, 1983.

———. *Essays in Physics*. New York: Philosophical Library, 1950.

———. *Ideas and Opinions*. New York: Bonanza, 1954.

———. *Out of My Later Years*. Secaucus, NJ: Citadel, 1956.

Ellis, Joseph J. *Founding Brothers: The Revolutionary Generation*. New York: Vintage, 2002.

Fineman, Howard. *The Thirteen American Arguments: Enduring Debates That Define and Inspire Our Country*. New York: Random House, 2008.

99

Gil, Anton. *An Honorable Defeat: A History of the German Resistance to Hitler, 1933–1945.* New York: Henry Holt, 1994.

Goodreads. Belief Quotes. https://www.goodreads.com/quotes/tag/belief.

Gregory, Bruce. *Inventing Reality: Physics as Language.* New York: Wiley, 1988.

Hagerty, Barbara Bradley. *Fingerprints of God: The Search for the Science of Spirituality.* New York: Riverhead, 2009.

Hall, Edward T. *Beyond Culture.* New York: Anchor, 1976.

Hoffmann, Banesh, and Helen Dukas. *Albert Einstein: Creator and Rebel.* New York: Plume, 1972.

James, William. The Will to Believe: An Address to the Philosophical Clubs of Yale and Brown Universities, 1896. https://arquivo.pt/wayback/20090714151749/ http://falcon.jmu.edu/~omearawm/ph101willtobelieve.html.

Kant, Immanuel. *Critique of Pure Reason.* Translated by F. Max Müller. New York: Anchor, 1966.

Kegan, Robert. *The Evolving Self: Problems and Process in Human Development.* Boston, MA: Harvard University Press, 1982.

Kliewer, Stephen P., and John Saultz. *Healthcare and Spirituality.* Oxford, UK: Radcliffe, 2006.

Lewis, C.S. *The Four Loves.* San Diego, CA: Harvest, 1960.

———. *Mere Christianity.* New York: Touchstone, 1996.

Mastin, Luke. *The Basics of Philosophy.* https://www.philosophybasics.com/.

Mazur, Joseph. *Euclid in the Rainforest: Discovering the Universal Truth in Logic and Mathematics.* New York: Pi, 2005.

Metaxas, Eric. *Bonhoeffer: Pastor, Martyr, Prophet, Spy.* Nashville, TN: Thomas Nelson, 2010.

Middlekauff, Robert. *The Glorious Cause: The American Revolution, 1763–1789.* Oxford, UK: Oxford University Press, 1982.

Moser, Paul K., ed. *The Oxford Handbook of Epistemology.* Oxford, UK: Oxford University Press, 2002.

Nagel, Jennifer. *Knowledge: A Very Short Introduction.* Oxford: Oxford University Press, 2014.

New Oxford American Dictionary. New York: Oxford University Press, 2010.

Popper, Karl. *Conjectures and Refutations.* New York: Routledge, 1963.

Robertson, Edwin, ed. *Dietrich Bonhoeffer: Selected Writings.* London: Fount, 1995.

Rothstein, Edward. *Emblems of the Mind: The Inner Life of Music and Mathematics.* New York: Times, 1995.

Simons, Richard C., and Herbert Pardes. *Understanding Human Behavior in Health and Illness.* Baltimore, MD: Williams and Wilkins, 1981.

Watzlawick, Paul, ed. *The Invented Reality: How Do We Know What We Believe We Know?* New York: W.W. Norton, 1984.

Wind, Renate. *Dietrich Bonhoeffer: A Spoke in the Wheel.* Grand Rapids, MI: William B. Eerdmans, 1992.

Index

www.ingramcontent.com/pod-product-compliance
Lightning Source LLC
Chambersburg PA
CBHW071838090426
42737CB00012B/2285